Dictionary of
Rail & Steam

BROCKHAMPTON PRESS
LONDON

© 1997 Geddes & Grosset Ltd,
David Dale House, New Lanark, Scotland.

All rights reserved. No part of this publication may be reproduced, stored in a retrieval system, or transmitted in any form or by any means, electronic, mechanical, photocopying, recording or otherwise, without the prior permission of the copyright holder.

This edition published 1997 by Brockhampton Press,
a member of Hodder Headline PLC Group.

1 86019 729 9

Printed and bound in India

Contents

Dictionary of Rail and Steam   9

Chronology of Rail and Steam   149

Preserved, Private and Tourist Railways 179

A

accommodation crossing
A level crossing provided by a landlord for his own and his tenants' private use where a section of his land has been divided by a railway.

Adams, William Bridges (1797–1872)
A British engineer who invented the railcar in 1843, the radial axlebox in 1863 and the rail FISHPLATE in 1847.

air brakes
A common braking system whereby the brakes are applied by the controlled release of compressed air.

allegheny
A US STEAM LOCOMOTIVE with 2–6–6–6 wheel arrangement.

amalgamation
During the years of the First World War, the railways had been coordinated by a Railway Executive Committee in an attempt to make them run as one system during the period of increased wartime demand. This committee was formed by the government by virtue of an Act of 1871 which empowered it to do so. Although the government did not attempt to administer the railways directly, it exerted considerable influence on the company managers who controlled the committee. Therefore, for the duration of the war, the railways were for the first time state-controlled, albeit indirectly.

The burden of providing the many additional services demanded by war and the resulting disruption to normal services

amalgamation

was not borne evenly by all the railway companies. Some bore a heavier responsibility for troop transportation, such as the South Western which carried more than 20 million soldiers to embarcation at Southampton, and the Highland, which provided the only access by rail to Scapa Flow and the Cromarty Firth, where two of the main naval bases were situated. The immense tasks faced by railways such as these could only be accomplished with considerable cooperation from other lines, particularly for the borrowing of rolling stock. However, it became clear that some lines were never likely to recover from their war effort. The Highland, for instance, ran over some very rough and sparsely populated terrain. How was it to raise capital to replace rolling stock damaged and worn out during the war years?

The war had, however, demonstrated the huge benefits afforded by cooperation between the railways. Amalgamation was not a new concept: between 1801 and 1914 some 1279 railway companies were incorporated, but as late as 1922, there were only 168 separate companies. Since the first amalgamation in 1834, a steady stream of small amalgamations had kept the numbers of companies comparatively low. However, it is not hard to imagine just how unwieldy a railway network run by 168 different companies might have been, each with its own safety standards and employment regulations, not to mention differences in fares and standards of comfort for passengers.

Furthermore, in the early years of this century, the railways were to come under increasing pressure from new modes of land transport—particularly the bus. Some railway companies were quick to realize the implications of this new form of public transport, and many seized upon the opportunity to buy buses which could be boarded from their own stations. Sadly, none invested enough in buses or electric trams, a decision which many came to regret. What was clear was that the public's inexorable drift away from the railways had begun, and that many small companies and unprofitable lines would cease to exist if something were not done to rationalize and update services.

Many favoured complete control over the railways by the state—nationalization—but this was not an attractive proposition to the Conservative/Liberal coalition government. Instead, a Ministry of Transport was established in 1919 to thrash out a new plan for the railways. Thus the Railways Act of 1921 was born—a bold and radical departure from the status quo. With the exception of 45 minor provincial companies, all companies were to be amalgamated into four main groups: the Southern, the Western, The North Western, Midland and West Scottish Group and the North Eastern and Eastern Scottish Group. When the grouping came into force on 1 January 1923, the new railway companies were known as:

1 The Great Western Railway
2 The London, Midland and Scottish Railway
3 The London and North Eastern Railway
4 The Southern Railway.

However, many of the pre-amalgamation problems still remained. Amalgamation did not eradicate competition—after all, the railways were still privately owned and were based very much on the old companies and consequently on old rivalries. The Ministry of Transport had not been successful in persuading the managers to break up any of the old companies, therefore the new groupings were often illogical and most certainly unequal in size and economic power, depending on the wealth of the new areas they served.

Although amalgamation did not achieve the kind of success the government had envisaged, it would be unfair to regard amalgamation as a total failure. The Southern Railway, for example, showed great enterprise under the guidance of Sir Herbert Walker. He oversaw substantial electrification and increase in passenger services, creating virtual suburbs of Portsmouth, Chatham and Brighton by 1939. His vastly improved rail services created a demand for suburban building, which in turn led to increased numbers of passengers and increased profits for the Southern. The larger companies, however, were reluctant to part with the considerable amounts of money which were required to electrify the main lines. Although this reluctance was due to some extent to conservatism, the companies were not without financial troubles. Labour problems, and strikes in particular, had hit them hard, and due to government legislation dating back a hundred years, they were not free to raise fares in order to recoup their losses. This may not have helped in any case, as they found themselves continually undercut by both the bus and, increasingly, the lorry.

Following the depression and slump of 1929–30, the railways were forced to cut many thousands of miles of unprofitable lines. In 1938, the railway companies prevailed upon the government to allow them to set their own fares, but Stanley Baldwin's government prevaricated and no decision had been reached by the outbreak of war. The government also failed to give a clear lead on transport policy or to help the railways compete with the increased use of motor transport which clearly benefits neither the railways nor public interest.

The amalgamation years were not without innovation and achievement. In addition to its radical programme of electrification, the Southern embarked upon an ambitious station rebuilding policy which provided the passenger with far superior facilities to any they had previously encountered. The Great Western, which had pioneered the development of automatic train control, installed it on all its main lines during these years, and was the only company to adopt the Continental model of diesel railcar use. The London and North Eastern made spectacular advances in the express train design—its locomotive MALLARD achieved 126 mph, a record unbeaten by a steam train. The London Midland and Scottish set about standardizing equipment and also made a brave foray into the development of British air services in order to allay the threat of competition.

What the railways lacked during these years was a clear sense of direction, adequate investment and an aggressive marketing policy. None of the management teams involved had really come to accept that the railways no longer enjoyed a monopoly of power, and were generally ill-suited to taking the bold steps required. It seems clear that the railways were fixed on a downward decline that neither government nor managements seemed able to arrest. The outbreak of the Second World War, however, was to change everything.

American
A US STEAM LOCOMOTIVE with 4–4–0 wheel arrangement.

American railways
The Americans were quick to catch on to early British developments and in 1829 four British STEAM LOCOMOTIVES were delivered to the Delaware and Hudson canal company. Unfortunately, the first outing for one of these engines was marred by the disintegration of the track, a setback which consigned the engines to storage, never to run for the Delaware and Hudson again.

Meanwhile, a wealthy New York philanthropist by the name of Peter Cooper had been attempting to persuade the owners of the BALTIMORE AND OHIO RAILROAD to use steam locomotives. His main difficulty was that Robert STEPHENSON himself had asserted that the track was unsuitable for steam locomotives due to a tight curve of 122 metre radius. Undaunted, Cooper responded to this challenge by building his own tiny steam engine which he christened Tom Thumb. The locomotive successfully hauled a carriage containing the directors of the Baltimore and Ohio Railway some 26 miles (42km) along the track and back.

American railways

As a result of this breakthrough, the Baltimore and Ohio held its own RAINHILL-type trials, but unfortunately American railway technology was so far behind that of Britain that the performance of home-grown models was more than disappointing. Imports of British models also generally resulted in failure, principally because of the lack of supporting technology. In Britain, track and other railway components were developing apace of locomotives, whereas in America the metal-capped wooden rails were unable to withstand the weight of the engines. Early failures clearly thwarted investment and experiment in steam locomotion—the Delaware and Hudson continued to use horsepower to haul its passenger service until 1860.

In time, however, these early problems were surmounted and a number of railway companies and an embryo network of lines began to emerge across the continent. As in Britain, there was at first no uniformity of gauge between the various states. In New England and the north, the British standard 1435mm gauge was in use, mainly to accommodate the first British engines in use there, but by 1861, more than 46% of the 50,000 miles (80,515 km) of track used gauges of differing widths. Not until 1886 was the national gauge finally standardized to 1435mm—at great inconvenience and cost to many railways.

In the 1850s the railways began to thrust westwards following the opening of the Galena to Chicago line in 1845. Within ten years, this single line had developed into the powerful Chicago and North Western Railway, heralding a period of massive boom and expansion in the American railway system. During this period, a plethora of railway companies were inaugurated from the eastern seaboard to the west coast.

During the American Civil War the railways played a significant logistic role. In fact, there seems little doubt that the final outcome of the war itself was directly affected by the railways' pattern of development. A rapidly expanding network of rail links from north eastern states to upper Mississippi and Ohio stood in sharp contrast to the eleven confederacy states whose lines amounted to less than one third of the country's total rail mileage. Furthermore, those confederate railway companies which did exist suffered a major wartime defection of personnel to the north. This happened because they had chosen to employ the technically superior Yankees on their railways.

The expansion of the railways reached its zenith in 1916 at which time the total network reached 249,433 miles (401,633km)—a figure which by 1979 had declined to 184,500 miles (297,100km) as a result of massive development in road and air transport this century. However, the decline of the railways was matched by growing popular concern about pollution and other environmental problems caused by the car. In a far-sighted and uncharacteristically non-capitalistic action, the American government sought to slow the decline of the railways by the creation of the passenger service AMTRAK in April 1971. A federally subsidized corporation, Amtrak today carries passengers over 23,600 miles (38,000km) of track.

Amsterdam to Harlem Railways
The Amsterdam to Harlem was the Netherlands' first railway. It opened on 24 September 1839.

Amtrak
Amtrak is an American public corporation which was set up in 1970 to run much of the passenger services including inter-city routes supported by public funds.

Apex
Cheap inter-city fares introduced in 1990. Apex enables the passenger to travel at a substantially reduced rate provided he purchases the ticket at least one week in advance of travel. However, the number of fares available is limited.

Argentinian railways

Argentina's first railway, which ran between Buenos Aires and Forista, opened on 30 August 1857. Its first locomotive had originally been intended for INDIAN RAILWAYS where 1676mm had been the standard GAUGE. For this reason, that same gauge was adopted on the new Argentinian railway, although by the Second World War, the Argentinian railway system totalled 28,600 miles (46,050km) of track on three different gauges.

In 1956, the railways were divided into six different groups, each bearing the name of a prominent person. The Mitre division, with its 1676mm gauge, consisted mainly of the old Central Argentinian Railway. The Buenos Aires Great Southern Railway, mainly 1676mm gauge but with 177 miles (285km) of 750mm gauge, became the Roca. The former Buenos Aires and Pacific Railway became the San Martin (1676mm gauge), whilst the Buenos Aires Western Railway became the Sarmiento (1676mm gauge). All those 1435mm lines built since 1864 constituted the Urquiza—formerly the Entre Rios, the Argentine north Eastern, the Central Buenos Aires and Argentine State Railways. Finally, those lines of 1000mm gauge, the earliest of which opened in 1887 (Cordoba Central) became the Belgrano division. In 1991, a directive was issued calling for the privatization of all systems. Passenger services have been much reduced, leaving only long-haul services from Buenos Aires.

Armstrong, Sir George (1822–1901)

Sir George Armstrong was one of the engineers on the GREAT WESTERN RAILWAY. In 1864, he became Locomotive Superintendent of the Northern Division based at Wolverhampton.

Arrol, Sir William (1839–1913)

Sir William Arrol was the civil engineering contractor most notably responsible for the second Tay Railway Bridge near Dundee. He also built the Queen Alexandra Bridge in Sutherland.

ASLEF
The Associated Society of Locomotive Engineers and Firemen is the train drivers' union, founded in 1880.

Aspinall, Sir John (1851–1907)
Sir John Aspinall was the Lancashire and Yorkshire Railway's chief mechanical engineer from 1886–1899 and later became their general manager. He was responsible for the completion of the Harwich locomotive works near Bolton. at that time state-of-the-art. He pioneered the standardization of locomotive components which could be employed in a variety of designs. He was also one of the early proponents of electrification in 1904 for the Liverpool to Southport line, and later supervised the electrification of the Manchester to Bury line in 1916.

Atlantic
US and British name for any STEAM LOCOMOTIVE having 4-4-2 wheel arrangement.

atmospheric railway
In this system, stationary pumping engines alongside the track operated to create a vacuum in a continuous pipe situated between the tracks. A piston located within the pipe connected to special carriages in the train by means of an arm running along a slot on the upper part of the tube. As the arm ran along the pipe, a continuous leather flap opened and closed to keep the pipe sealed. As the vacuum was created within the pipe, the piston was drawn along the tube hauling the train along the track. The atmospheric railway did enjoy some success—between 1843 and 1855 an Irish line between Kingstown and Dalkey pulled trains at speeds of up to 57mph (92.5km/h), and atmospheric railways from Forest Hill to Croydon and in south Devon operated for a short period in the mid-19th century. Atmospheric railways suffered from various technical problems which

could not be solved by the available technology, and in any case their performance was easily superseded by developments in steam traction. A working model of an atmospheric railway still exists at the Atmospheric Railway Museum, Starcross, Devon.

Australian railways

The development of Australian railways was somewhat fragmented, each colony proceeding with its own construction programme without thought for the consequences of possible unification at some point in the future. Australia's first steam-driven railway opened between Melbourne and Sandridge in Victoria on 1600mm gauge track on 12 September 1854. However, by the time of the Constitution of the Australian Commonwealth in 1900, Australia had 12,500 miles (20,128km) of track consisting of three different gauges. Since the early 1900s, most new lines have been built to the standard 1435mm gauge. The Second World War demonstrated the need for unification, but it happened only gradually as a result of cost and the frequent involvement of vast distances.

From the early days of Australian Railways, the separate colonies' administrations had a greater involvement in their construction and operation than in many other countries. This was mainly because they were frequently required to bail companies out of financial difficulties or provide some incentive to get railways built in the first place. (Railway construction was not always an attractive proposition in Australia, as so many of the larger population centres were bounded by sea on one side and vast expanses of desert on the other.) Today, there are six railway systems owned by the government and operated by the following bodies:

1 State Railway Authority of New South Wales
2 Queensland Government Railways
3 Victorian Railways

4 Western Australian Government Railways
5 State Transport authority of South Australia
6 Australian National Railways.

automatic signalling
A system in which the signals are triggered and changed to stop (normally they lie in clear mode) by the passage of the train. This gives protection to that particular section of track as long as the train is still within it.

automatic train
A train which in normal operation is controlled entirely by electronic systems and has no active driver.

automatic warning system
This system warns a driver of clear and caution warnings on the signals by audible means and automatically applies the brakes if the driver fails to acknowledge the warning.

axle counter
These devices are situated at the entrance and exit of block sections in the track and record the number of axles passing over it. The signalling apparatus is locked whilst there is a train in its block section and will not unlock until it has checked the same number of axles have quit the section, thereby ensuring that only one train can occupy a block at any given time.

B

backing signal
A SEMAPHORE signal arm that regulates wrong direction operating within station limits.

backplate
The plate situated to the rear of the BOILER and FIREBOX on a STEAM LOCOMOTIVE upon which are located various controls including the REGULATOR and gauges

Baker Street and Waterloo Railway
Incorporated in 1893, the Baker Street and Waterloo Railway was an UNDERGROUND RAILWAY that connected the two London stations which give it its name. Its first section opened in 1906, and it eventually extended from Queen's Park to Elephant and Castle.

Baker, Sir Benjamin (1840–1907)
Sir Benjamin Baker was a civil engineer whose greatest triumph is the famous Forth Railway Bridge completed in 1890. He was also involved in the construction of the first UNDERGROUND rail system in London.

Balaclava railway
The Balaclava was the first ever military railway built by the British. Constructed in 1855, it ran as a supply route from the port of Balaclava to the front during the Crimean War.

ballast
The small stones used as a bed for the track SLEEPERS. Clinker, shingle and slag are occasionally substituted.

ballast train
A train which was built to bring and distribute new ballast to the track. Originally used as a term to describe any engineer's train.

Baltic
Initially an American term used to describe a STEAM LOCOMOTIVE with a 4–6–4 wheel arrangement, later also adopted in Britain.

Baltimore and Ohio Railroad
The Baltimore and Ohio Railroad was the first railway in North

America, incorporated in 1827. Its first section opened between Ellicot's mills, Maryland and Baltimore on 24 May, 1830, initially using horse traction. Robert Stephenson had initially dissuaded the Baltimore and Ohio from using steam traction on the line as he believed that curves on the track necessitated by the terrain were too sharp to be safely negotiated by a STEAM LOCOMOTIVE. The philanthropist, Peter Cooper, was determined to prove him wrong. He built his own steam engine, the diminutive Tom Thumb, which successfully hauled a wagon carrying the directors of the Baltimore and Ohio some 13 miles (8km).

banker, banking engine
An extra engine linked to a train at either front or rear to assist in pulling it up a steep bank.

barrier vehicles
Often an empty coach, wagon or van is used to act as a barrier between the locomotive and a hazardous load. Occasionally barrier vehicles are situated at either end of a train or between the brake van and the locomotive.

baseplate
A plate secured under a sleeper which forms a locating device for flat-bottomed rails. Spring clips are used to attach the rail to the baseplate.

Basel to St Louis railway
The Basel to St Louis was the first railway to open in Switzerland. It opened on 15 June 1844.

bay
Typically found in a through station, a bay is a kind of short platform with buffer stops usually found at opposite sides or ends of a normal sized platform. They are normally used for branch lines or services which terminate at the station.

Beeching, Dr Richard (1913–85)

Dr Richard Beeching was the much maligned chairman of BRITISH RAIL (BR) in the 1960s whose custodianship has been remembered for the drastic cuts in railway mileage, services and staff. The Transport Act of 1962 had relieved the British Rail of the burden of the interest on an accumulated debt of £1,175,000,000 and allowed it more freedom to fix charges than it had ever enjoyed in the past. However, these concessions came with the proviso that the railways were to concentrate on services which were deemed to be profitable, and to this end, Dr Beeching's new Railway Board produced the first of two reports: *The Reshaping of British Railways*.

This report identified the most unprofitable and indeed loss-making aspects of British Rail. For instance, the report exposed that of Britain's 7000 stations, approximately half of these produced only 2% of the total passenger revenue. Similarly, half the number of freight stations were producing only 3% of the total traffic. It transpired that those stations least used by the network were costing somewhere in the region of £9,000,000 per annum. Clearly, the social costs of closing those lines and stations which were deemed to be unprofitable had to be balanced against considerations of profitability, and the report discussed at length how best the impact of the closures might be softened.

Many were vociferous in the condemnation of Dr Beeching and his report, especially those who stood to lose their services, as well as railway employees likely to lose their jobs. By 1965, many of Dr Beeching's proposals for closure had been implemented, although these were halted by the incoming Labour government, and by 1968 more than thirty per cent of the route mileage had been closed. For this, Beeching had to endure much personal vilification in his lifetime, whereas his Board's second report *The Development of the Major Railway Trunk*

Roads has been largely ignored by his many detractors. This report embodied real vision for the future of British Rail, and while he accepted that most European railways were never going to be hugely profitable, a balance could be struck between a profitable commercial sector, and the numerous services which would always require government support.

Although almost all of Beeching's recommendations in the second report were adopted, Beeching's vision for the railways has sadly never been realized. Every measure taken to reduce unprofitable lines involving redeployment of labour or redundancy has been met with costly industrial action, thereby delaying the introduction of new services and technology.

Belpaire

The Belpaire was a popular type of FIREBOX for STEAM LOCOMOTIVES invented by the Belgian engineer Alfred Jules BELPAIRE in 1860–64.

Belpaire, Alfred Jules (1820–1903)

Belpaire was the Belgian locomotive engineer who designed the famous Belpaire FIREBOX favoured by many locomotive builders.

Beyer, Charles Frederick (1813–1876)

Beyer was a locomotive engineer and manufacturer. Originally from Saxony, he settled in Manchester as a designer for Sharp, Roberts and Co. Together with Richard PEACOCK, he founded the famous Beyer Peacock locomotive building firm in 1854. Beyer Peacock went on to supply locomotives for many railway companies around the world.

Bidder, George Parker (1806–76)

Bidder was an eminent civil engineer and mathematician who contributed to the laying out of many of the early British Railways, including the Great Eastern. He also advised on the Belgian railway system. He and Robert STEPHENSON together constructed the Oslo to Eidsvoll Railway, the first in Norway. As a consultant to the fledgling INDIAN RAILWAYS, he was responsible for the adoption of the 1676mm gauge.

Blenkinsop, John (1783–1831)

John Blenkinsop was one of the early British STEAM LOCOMOTIVE pioneers who designed a system of toothed wheel and rack or cog railway. Teeth were cast into the side of the rail in order to mesh with a toothed cog wheel driven by the engine. A mechanical engineer from Leeds, Matthew MURRAY built four locomotives to Blenkinsop's design which went on to work for twenty years in the Middleton Colliery Railway near Leeds.

block system

The system of signalling in which the line is divided into discrete sections or blocks, into which only one train is permitted at any given time. Each section has a signal box at each end, and signalmen communicate with their colleagues in adjacent boxes by means of electric block telegraph instruments which can indicate train on the line, line blocked, or line clear. These are used in conjunction with sound signals (bell codes) which describe the types of train.

block train (1)

A train which always runs as a whole unit, i.e. is not uncoupled in normal use.

block train (2)

A freight train which remains unchanged between departure and arrival at its destination.

bloomers

The first of the 'bloomer' locomotives was built by J. E. McConnell in 1861. They were named after, Amelia Bloomer, the first woman to wear trousers, because, like her legs, their wheels were visible (due to the absence of frames outside them).

Blucher
Blucher was an early locomotive by George STEPHENSON which ran on the rack and cog system at Killingworth in 1814.

Board of Trade
The government department responsible for the railways and tramways from its creation in 1840 until the Ministry of Transport was formed in 1919.

boat train
A train operated specifically to connect with sailings or arrivals of a shipping service.

bogie
The bogie four-wheeled truck at the front of a locomotive which supported much of the weight of the BOILER and smokebox and also helped with the steering. Its frame pivoted from a cross member of the locomotive's main frame, and its side movement was controlled by springs which returned the bogie to its correct position on a central pivot if it had been displaced.

boiler
To make the wheels of a locomotive turn, boiling water is required to provide the steam which, under pressure will ultimately turn the wheels. Steam engines most often had boiler made of rings of steel plate fused together. In order to boil the water, the boiler is connected to a FIREBOX which contains the coal fire. This usually consists of an inner and outer firebox, but many variations in design have attempted to maximize efficiency. For example, some engines had ducts (thermic syphons) which permitted the circulation of water within the firebox itself, and some boilers were tapered with the widest part at the

firebox end. This would allow for maximum heating whilst cutting down on steel and weight.

Within the boiler are approximately 158–180 flue tubes. Hot gases from the firebox pass through these tubes which distribute the heat throughout the water, and the resultant steam collects in a space at the top of the boiler above the water level. The dome, which is clearly visible from the outside of the engine, contains a steam collector which serves to direct the steam through the regulator valve into the CYLINDERS. (The regulator valve is controlled by the driver.) The pressure of steam in the boiler typically ranges from 200–250lbs (91–113 kg) per square inch. While the engine is working, the fireman is responsible for checking the pressure in the boiler by monitoring the gauge glasses in the cab. When required, he will operate the injectors, thereby forcing high-velocity jet of steam and water from the TENDER into the boiler, via non-return clack valves. When the pressure within the boiler exceeds the maximum safety level, the excess is released through safety valves.

Some boilers are equipped with SUPERHEATERS, which can raise the temperature of the steam by approximately 250° F (121°C) Enlarged flue tubes contain the superheating elements, and the steam will travel along these tubes towards the firebox and back before going on to power the cylinders. This greatly increases the pressure of the steam.

bolster

A transverse member on a truck separated from the BOGIE by means of springs and shock-absorbing devices. It supports the weight of the car body.

bolster wagon

An open FREIGHT wagon with raised transverse beams which keep the load free of the floor enabling easy loading and unloading.

Bolton and Leigh Railway
The Bolton and Leigh in Lancashire opened on 1 August 1828 using steam traction.

booking office
The office from which rail travel tickets are purchased. The term has survived fro the days of the stagecoach when all passenger transactions were required to be entered in a book.

bow collector
A uni-directional current collector which slides along overhead electric wires collecting current for either trains or trams. It is shaped like a bow, hence the name.

BR *see* BRITISH RAIL.

bracket arm
A tubular steel arm attached to a traction pole at right angles from which the overhead wires of a tramway are suspended.

brake composite
A coach which can accomodate both first and second class passengers as well as a guard's and a luggage compartment.

brake pin
An iron pin which secures the wagon brake when the brake handle is pushed down.

brake road
A siding where brake vans are stored.

brake stick
A pole used to force down wagon brake handles by shunters.

brakes
Until 1870, most railways were still reliant upon mechanically operated brakes. To the rear of a passenger train the brakeman

brakes

in his brake van would pull frantically at his brake lever upon hearing a whistled signal from the driver. The locomotive itself was fitted with brakes, but on most railways the only supplement to these were the block-brakes operated by the brakeman. However, accident after accident dictated that continuous and automatic brakes be used on passenger trains, so that any vehicle which became detached from the body of the train would brake immediately. Continuous brakes throughout the length of the train became law when the Railways Regulation Act was passed in 1889, although this development applied only to passenger trains.

The lack of continuous brakes consigned goods vehicles to trundling around the country at ridiculously slow speeds. As passenger trains attained ever increasing speeds, goods trains became more and more of a nuisance. However, none of the private companies could bear the cost of fitting all their freight trains with continuous brakes. Some circumvented the problem to a certain extent—the Midland tried to keep its freight trains on separate tracks, whilst the GREAT WESTERN RAILWAY fitted a few of its goods trains in express service with continuous brakes. All in all, little progress was made until nationalization of the railways in 1948. The BRITISH TRANSPORT COMMISSION had half of the old companies' freight wagons scrapped and only then could the brake problem be seriously addressed. The Modernization Plan of 1955 set out to do just that and by 1959 almost a third of the remaining freight trains had been fitted with continuous brakes. However, until the 1970s, the majority of freight trains still had a brake van with mechanical brakes operated by a guard at the rear of the train.

Another problem lay in the type of brakes adopted. Following trials at Newark in 1875, most railways adopted the British-invented vacuum brake system in preference to the American Westinghouse air-brake system. The vacuum system proved unequal to the task with the advent of high-speed passenger trains in the 1960s, and British Rail were saddled with the huge cost of converting to air brakes.

brakesman
A guard on a freight train.

Brazilian railways
The first railway to open in Brazil ran from Mana (Bay of Rio) to the Petropolis Serra on 30 April 1854 with a gauge of 1676mm. It was later to become part of the Leopoldina Railway with an eventual total of 1900 miles (3060km).

Brazil's federal railways became joint-stock companies in 1957 under Ríde Ferroviaria Federal SA, the holding company. Today, this is divided into twelve regionally operated systems and the Brazilian Urban Train Company (Companhia Brasiliera de Trens Urbanos), the suburban and metro system operators. In addition to these, there is also the state-operated Ferrovia Paulista, an amalgamation of five São Paulo Railways. This system is mostly concerned with the transport of bulk freight with a much reduced commitment to passenger services since 1976. However, São Paulo suburban services are still responsible for about 110 million passenger journeys. There are also three smaller railways, mainly for freight—the Estrada de Ferro Carajas, the Estrada de Ferro do Amapò, and the Estrada de Ferro Vitûria a Minas.

breakaway
A train which has become divided accidentally.

breakdown
A train kept in readiness at a depot in case of accident, derailment or breakdown. It is fully equipped with lifting gear, tool vans and accommodation for the crew and workers.

British Rail
British Rail was the title bestowed upon the new national railway system upon NATIONALIZATION in January 1948.

British Rail Engineering Ltd
British Rail Engineering Ltd manufactured all kinds of rolling stock. It was originally a subsidiary of the BRITISH RAILWAYS BOARD, but sold off as a private undertaking in 1989.

British Railways Board
The British Railways Board took over responsibility for running the railways from the BRITISH TRANSPORT COMMISSION in 1963. Formed by the Transport Act of 1962, the British Railways Board enjoyed almost total commercial freedom.

British Transport Commission
The British Transport Commission was formed in 1947 by the Transport Act of that year to administer the nationalized railway system (and all other forms of nationalized transport on the mainland). It handed over control of the railways to the BRITISH RAILWAYS BOARD in 1963.

British Transport Hotels
When the BRITISH TRANSPORT COMMISSION inherited all the hotels of the former railway companies upon nationalization in 1948, it originated its Hotels Executive. In 1953, this became a division of British Transport Hotels known as British Transport Hotels and Catering Services. In 1958, British Transport Hotels and Catering Services had responsibility for 36 hotels and 356 refreshment rooms as well as 700 restaurant and buffet cars daily. This responsibility continued under British Transport Hotels Ltd, registered in 1962, as well as all station catering facilities, restaurant car services and all laundry services for the railways and hotels. In 1963, British Transport Hotels became a subsidiary of the BRITISH RAILWAYS BOARD. By the end of 1983,

however, all the hotels belonging to the railways had been sold to private enterprise as part of the Conservative government's privatization plans. Prior to this, British Transport Hotels had been separated from other railway catering in 1982, and train catering became the sole responsibility of the British Railways Board.

broad gauge
Any GAUGE wider than the standard, or Stephenson gauge of 1435mm.

brogden joint
A special joint used for laying long rails. A 228mm vertical cut is made in the centre of the rail. Half the rail is cut away and the other half overlaps half of the adjoining rail. This ensures all the wheel treads have a continuous bearing surface.

Brunel, Isambard Kingdom (1806–59)
Son of civil engineer Marc Isambard Brunel (1769–1849), Isambard Kingdom Brunel trained with his father on the construction of the Thames Tunnel which was completed in 1842. At the age of 27, he was appointed chief engineer to the GREAT WESTERN RAILWAY (GWR) with its 2134mm gauge. Brunel exerted a major influence in railway engineering, and his extensions to the GWR included many bridges, tunnels and sections of track which were seen as daringly original in their day but have, in the main, stood the test of time. Perhaps the most famous of his civil engineering works is the Clifton suspension bridge which spans the Avon Gorge, to the west of Bristol, and the Royal Albert bridge, built across the Tamar estuary from Saltash into the south-western county of Cornwall.

buffet car
A coach on a train where some sort of catering is providing. This usually consists of a counter where hot and cold drinks and

snacks are dispensed, with a small kitchen for preparation. Occasionally there may be seating and tables.

bulkhead
The full-width partition at the end of the vehicle which usually has a door.

Bulleid, Oliver Vaughan Snell (1892–1970)
Bulleid was a disciple of Henry Ivatt's on the Great Northern Railway until 1912 when he became an assistant to Sir Herbert Gresley. In 1937, he became chief mechanical engineer at the Southern Railway where he packed many innovative and idiosyncratic design features into his 0–6–0 and 4–6–2 locomotives. He moved to Dublin in 1949 as chief mechanical engineer on Irish Railways, where his most notable achievement was to build a locomotive which used turf as fuel.

bullet trains
The name often given to the trains on the Japanese Shinkansen high-speed passenger services.

bullhead rail
A type of parallel rail with a larger upper surface upon which run the train's wheels. In Britain, the bullhead has now been all but superseded by the flat-bottom rail.

bunker
The coal container situated to the rear of a tank engine.

Burma–Thailand Railway
During the Second World War, the Japanese forced British (and other) prisoners of war to work on a railway connecting Burma with Thailand. The atrocious conditions under which they were made to work were dramatized in the film *The Bridge Over the River Kwai* and indeed many lost their lives. The railway itself was completed in October 1943.

Bury, Edward (1794–1858)
Bury founded a works to design and build locomotives in Liverpool and developed the bar frame construction which became standard in North American locomotive design. He was also responsible for the locomotives of the LONDON AND BIRMINGHAM RAILWAY and the Great Northern Railway. He built small, four-wheeled locomotives, and it was the underpricing of a series of 2–2–2s for the Lancashire and Yorkshire which resulted in the closure of his firm in 1850.

C

cab
The cab, situated to the rear of the STEAM LOCOMOTIVE, housed the driver and the fireman. It contained all controls and gauges for operating the locomotive—pressure gauges, REGULATOR controls and brake lever. It also contained the entrance to the FIREBOX into which the fireman would shovel coal from the TENDER behind the locomotive, and the injector control with which the fireman topped up water levels in the BOILER.

Caledonian Railway
The Caledonian Railway opened on 15 February 1848 and ran from Carlisle to Edinburgh and Glasgow. It completed the West Coast route although only a small portion of the journey is actually on the west coast. From 1923 onwards, it belonged to the LONDON, MIDLAND AND SCOTTISH RAILWAYS.

camber
A camber is created where one rail lies higher than the other to facilitate higher speeds on curves.

Canadian railways

The first steam railway to be built in Canada ran from Laprairie to St John on 21 July 1836 on 1435mm GAUGE. The owners of this enterprise were The Company of Proprietors of the Champlain and St Lawrence Rail Road, and as more companies gradually followed their lead, the old gauge problem began to raise its ugly head. The Albion Colliery Tramway and the Erie and Ontario followed suit with 1435mm in 1839, but the Montreal and Lachine railroad opened for business with a gauge of 1448mm. In 1845, a Royal Commission was appointed by the Province of Canada (Ontario and Quebec) to consider the vexed question of the gauge, but as they deliberated, the St Lawrence and Atlantic Rail Road opened their link from Montreal to Portland, Maine, USA with a gauge of 1676mm.

Flying in the face of professional opposition to the broad gauge, the committee finally recommended its adoption with the Guarantee Act of 1849. The broad gauge became known as the 'provincial gauge' and only those companies which adopted it were entitled to financial assistance. This meant that by 1860 92% of Canadian public railway (including the Province of Canada, Nova Scotia and New Brunswick) were broad gauge, despite continuing strong opposition from the companies and the engineers. When the Great Western Railway built its line from Niagara Falls to Windsor, Ontario, it initially built to the regulation 1676mm gauge, but later incorporated a third line to provide it with standard gauge.

By the time New Brunswick, Nova Scotia Quebec and Ontario had been united into the Dominion of Canada (1867), there already existed 15 railways covering a total of 2495 miles (4017 km). The Dominion government finally repealed the Provincial gauge in 1870, as by this time most of the US and Canadian lines were using standard gauge.

Canadian National Railways was formed by the government

to assist the Canadian Northern Railway which was experiencing serious financial difficulty in 1919. Gradually, it absorbed other railways, including the Grand Trunk and the Newfoundland. Today, it covers about 21,330 miles (34,347km), providing a service for all ten provinces. It also owns a highway transport service, steamships, a large hotel chain and a telecommunications service. Air Canada is a subsidiary of CNR.

Canadian Pacific Railway was incorporated on 15 February 1881 to build the first transcontinental Canadian line from Port Moody to Montreal. The building of this line within ten years had been a condition of British Columbia's confederation into the Dominion of Canada in 1871. Work began in May 1881 and was completed in November 1885, although the first transcontinental services did not commence until June 1886. Today, Canadian Pacific Ltd is a huge concern operating six departments. CP Rail still operates 14,869 miles (23,943km) of the old CPR network and CP Transport is Canada's largest road haulier. The other departments are CP Telecommunications, CP Hotels and CP Air.

British Columbia Railway still operates 1281 miles (2062km) of track in the West of Canada, whilst the Ontario Northland Railway and the Quebec North Shore and Labrador Railway still operate various passenger and freight services.

Via Rail was set up in 1976, and eventually bought all CN and CP Rail passenger equipment in an attempt to revitalize passenger services. In April 1979, Via was able to assume full financial responsibility for all former CN and CP Rail passenger services. It now operates more than 8583 miles (13,822km) of route.

Canterbury and Whitstable Railway
The Canterbury and Whitstable was the first to operate a normal passenger service using steam power. It opened on 3 May 1830,

and used two stationary engines for the first four miles and a locomotive for the last two. Its first class carriages were virtually identical to stage coaches, although built with stronger iron frames.

cape gauge
A 1067mm (3ft 6in) gauge, so called because of its use in South Africa. *See also* SOUTH AFRICAN RAILWAYS.

capuchon
A specially designed raised lip situated at the front of the chimney on a STEAM LOCOMOTIVE. It kept smoke and exhaust away from the windows of the cab and prevented down draught.

car carrier
As the name suggests, a train which conveys passengers and their cars. It is now better known as Motorail.

car miles
A unit of measurement which describes one rail car moving over one mile of line.

carriage dock
A short platform used for loading military or road vehicles onto wagons or vans. The end would have a ramp from the train to road level.

Catch Me who Can
Catch Me who Can was built by Richard TREVITHICK in 1808 and has been reconstructed using surviving drawings. Trevithick is credited with designing the first ever working STEAM LOCOMOTIVE in 1804, which successfully hauled a train carrying coal wagons and 70 passengers.

catch points
These are points which are designed to derail a train travelling

in the wrong direction without damaging it. They are found on slopes and are compulsory where the gradient is greater than 1 in 260. If the gradient is long, a second pair must be added.

catenary
The cable and hangers which support conductor wire for overhead electric traction systems.

centipede
An American STEAM LOCOMOTIVE with 2–12–0 wheel arrangement.

chair
The cast iron fitting fixed to a sleeper into which bullhead rails are fitted. The rails are secured by means of a wooden key.

Champlain and St Lawrence Railway
The Champlain and St Lawrence opened between Laprairie and St John on 21 July 1836—the first steam railway in Canada. Its first locomotive was the Dorchester built by STEPHENSON & Co. The line was a land link in an otherwise uninterrupted water route from Montreal to New York.

Channel Tunnel
Proposals to build a channel tunnel were made as early as 1802, when a French mining engineer suggested that the tunnel should surface on an island in the middle of the channel constructed for changing horses. The second proposal, again by a Frenchman, was for a tunnel large enough to take two steam trains. Both of these schemes necessitated the building of ventilation shafts to above sea level, but in the event, neither were realized.

Since these early proposals, progress with the tunnel has been rather slow. In 1874, the South Eastern Railway obtained permission to sink experimental shafts. In 1875, the French and British governments agreed to the principal of the tunnel, and companies were formed to undertake the work. Between 1875 and 1881, about 2.5 miles (1.55km) of tunnel were actually built from both sides, but over the next 80 years of the tunnel's construction was characterized by dozens of feasibility reports and studies, but no actual tunnelling. The British government dropped out of the project entirely in 1975.

The issue was brought to life again in 1977 by the European Parliament which favoured a new viability study. In Britain, in 1981, an all-party committee of MPs voted in favour of constructing a 7-metre diameter tunnel. Initially, the French dragged their heels in view of previous British behaviour, but in 1986, a commitment was made by both sides and tunnelling commenced once more in earnest.

The two sides finally met in 1991—the first time Britain had been joined to France for 10,000 years. The tunnel was officially opened in 1994 by President Mitterand of France and Queen Elizabeth II.

Channel Tunnel Rail Link

The railway which connects London and the Channel tunnel.

Chapélon, Andre (1892–1978)

Chapélon was a French locomotive engineer whose developments brought steam locomotion to the zenith of its achievement. Chapélon was recruited by the Paris–Orleans Railway in the mid 1920s primarily to discover why it was that their Pacific 4-6-2 engines seemed unable to improve upon the performance of their Atlantic 4-6-0 engines. He decided to concentrate initially on thermodynamic principles, and culminated in a revision and expansion of some of CHURCHWARD's theories on the flow of steam. By refining and enlarging the steam passages, modifying valves and draughting, he achieved a staggering 50% increase in engine output from a 1929 specimen Paris–Orleans Pacific.

Working alongside Kylala of Finland, Chapélon also contributed significantly to the development of a new exhaust system (the KYLCHAP as it became known) with its double blastpipe and chimney. The kylchap represented a massive improvement in locomotive efficiency by increasing draught and minimizing back pressure.

His work exerted a profound influence on STEAM LOCOMOTIVE engineers throughout the world (most notably in Britain) and his engine No. 242 A1 recorded some simply stunning performances which ranked it among the greatest ever built.

check rail
At rail and road crossings an additional check rail is added inside the two normal rails as a guide for wheel FLANGES. A check rail is also used to keep wheels on the rails at viaducts, bridges and curves.

Cheltenham Flyer
This was an express train which was introduced to run between London and Cheltenham Spa in 1923 by the GREAT WESTERN RAILWAY. Although the title never enjoyed official status, the train became the fastest in regular service in Britain with speeds of 90mph. In 1931, the GWR officially claimed it as 'The World's Fastest Train.' The locomotive was a 4–6–0 Castle type designed by C. B. Collet, engineer on the GWR.

Chemin de Fer Métropolitain de Paris
The full title of the Métro or Paris UNDERGROUND RAILWAY system, the first section of which was opened in 1900.

Chesapeake
An American STEAM LOCOMOTIVE with 2–8–8–2 wheel arrangement first introduced on the Chesapeake and Ohio Railway.

children's railways
Some former communist countries built miniature railways for

children to provide them with practical training for a possible future career on the railways.

Chilean railways

The first railway to open in Chile (25 December 1851) ran from Caldera to Copiapo on 1435mm GAUGE tracks. The State opened its first railway on 1676mm BROAD-GAUGE track from Valparaiso to Santiago on 14 September 1863. This gauge stretched southwards to Puerto Montt, but to the north, railway development was on metre gauge. Eventually, the entire system was taken over by the state.

Chilean State Railways (EFE—Empresa de los Ferrocarriles des Estrado de Chile) divided the system into three autonomous parts in 1981. In 1987 divided it again into five operating divisions. It was decided in 1989 that the northern section, with its metre gauge, should run FREIGHT services only.

Chinese Railways

Naturally suspicious and mistrusting of all things British, it was not until 1876 that the Chinese permitted a British firm, Jardine Matheson, to open a line from Shanghai to Woosung. Initially, the locals were thrilled with the railway, but a fatal accident involving a labourer brought the joy to an abrupt end. The railway was dismantled and sent to Formosa, where it was left to rust.

Following this inauspicious beginning, there was little enthusiasm for rail in China for quite some time, although a permanent railway did open between Tongshan and Hsukuchang in 1880, and was later extended to Lutai and Tsientsin in 1888. Futher progress was negligible until the country was defeated in the Sino-Japanese War in 1895, an event which forced the administration to wake up to the benefits of rail transport. Attempts were made by the government to expand the pitiful rail network, but most of the money had to be borrowed, resulting in heavy European, American and Russian involvement. Many of the lines were badly constructed, and frequently failed to bridge large gaps caused by rivers and gorges. When the Japanese invaded again in 1935 it became obvious that the system was still a long way from coping with the demands of wartime transport.

At the time of the establishment of the People's Republic of China, in 1949, there was a mere 6830 miles (11,000km) of rail track in operation. Since then, great progress has been made with between 500 and 620 miles (800 and 1000km) of track on average added to the track each year, the costs of which have been borne by the Chinese government. An ongoing programme of improvement has resulted in old single lines being replaced by modern double-tracked routes, and high-speed lines forging through some of the highest mountain routes in the world. Programmes of electrification and conversion of the track to manganese steel are making good progress.

church interval

In the early days of the railways, respect for Sunday worship was shown by some London Rail operators by suspending all services for the duration of church services. First observed by the London and Greenwich Railway in 1836, the tradition of the church interval was not finally abandoned by all London train operators until 1926.

Churchward, George Jackson (1857–1933)

Churchward was a mechanical engineer (and later chief mechanical engineer) with the GREAT WESTERN RAILWAY. His unique talent was to evaluate current world locomotive practice and utilize and amalgamate its best elements. For instance, he combined the American-style tapered boiler shell with a Belgian BELPAIRE BOILER to great effect. Before making the decision to abandon compound engines completely, Churchward had three DE GLEHN compound ATLANTICS delivered to GWR in order that proper comparisons could be made with simple-expansion

Atlantics. His use of SUPERHEATING and long-travel piston valves demonstrated that his grasp of the available technology and willingness to experiment was years in advance of any of his peers.

circus train
A train designed to accommodate all the equipment, animals and performers of a circus, mainly found in the USA.

clayliner
A wagon designed specifically to carry china clay.

clearance/depression bar
A bar on the tracks which is interlocked to the signals. The bar is located at platforms and junctions and ensures the signals remain 'off' unless the bar is raised. The bar cannot be lifted as long as it has a vehicle on it.

clearing point
In BLOCK SYSTEM working, the line must be free of obstruction in order for a signalman to permit the approach of another train. The clearing point is that point to which the line must be clear ahead of the first outer home/stop signal, normally a distance of 400 metres.

clerestory
The central section of the roof of a coach raised and fitted with deck lights and ventilators to provide extra light and ventilation.

clockface service
A service whereby trains depart at the same number of minutes past each hour throughout the day, thereby obviating the need for passengers to read timetables.

coaching stock
The name given to all vehicles used to form passenger trains whether or not they actually carry passengers.

coal pusher
A device consisting of a large steam piston which pushes the coal forward in the TENDER, thus reducing the fireman's workload.

coal stage
A platform from which coal is loaded onto locomotives.

colour-light system
An electric signal issuing a powerful beam which is easily visible night and day, penetrating fog yet still remaining visible in bright sunshine.

Columbia
An American STEAM LOCOMOTIVE with 2–4–2 wheel arrangement.

comfort stop
A scheduled stop on a journey, made specifically to permit train crews to use lavatories at stations or depots.

commencemant and termination indicators
Illuminated indicators situated at the side of the line to show where a temporary speed limit starts and ends.

common carriers
Until the Transport Act of 1962, the British railways were known as common carriers because they were obliged to relay any goods or FREIGHT offered by the customer.

commuters
This was originally an American term applied to those who held a commutation or season ticket for a railway. It was adopted in Britain in the 1950s and was eventually extended to include any individual who had to travel by any form of transport from a suburban or rural home into a city-centre workplace.

Compagnie Internationale des Wagons-Lits
The International Sleeping Car Company was founded in 1876

and operated international PULLMAN, dining and sleeping car services until 1971. It operated in Europe, Asia and Russia (until the revolution in 1917) and still provides sleeping cars, catering services (rail and air) and hotels in Europe and Morocco.

company train
A freight train regularly in use for one particular customer.

compartment
A section of a coach in a passenger train which is partitioned off to allow two rows of up to six seats, the number depending upon the class of travel and the need to allow space for a corridor.

compensated gradient
In order to prevent the resistance caused by the combination of a curve and a gradient exceeding that of the resistance occasioned by a straight road gradient, the engineer will design a compensated gradient to ease the gradient over a curve on a steep incline.

composite
A composite coach is one which contains accommodation for more than one class of passenger.

compound steam engines
In most steam engines, the CYLINDERS were fed with steam which came directly from the boiler. These cylinders were described as high pressure. At the end of each complete piston movement, steam was normally exhausted to the atmosphere, but in the compound system, this spent steam was directed to another, larger low-pressure cylinder before being exhausted. The French engineer Alfred George DE GLEHN pioneered the development of the compound engine, the first of which was built in 1866 for the Nord Railway in France. Although very popular elsewhere in the world, these locomotives only achieved limited

success in Britain, perhaps as a result of restrictions posed on the size of the low-pressure cylinders by the standard gauge and LOADING GAUGE.

condensing locomotive

A STEAM LOCOMOTIVE fitted with a device intended to divert some of the exhaust fumes to the water tanks where working in tunnels (particularly in London, Glasgow or Liverpool) in an attempt to improve the atmosphere.

conductor rail

An electrified rail situated in the centre or at the side of the running rails. The current is collected by a shoe on the locomotive.

connecting rod

The connecting rod connects the pistons to the crank axle on a locomotive. It enables the backwards and forwards motion of the piston to be converted to the circular motion of the crankaxle and wheels.

Consolidation

An American locomotive with a 2–8–0 wheel arrangement.

container

A large tank or storage box for carrying freight which is interchangeable with trains and road vehicles, enabling the two methods of transport to be combined.

continental location

A method of describing wheel arrangement on steam locomotives by counting the axles rather than the wheels. Therefore a 4–4–2 in Whyte's notation would become a 2–2–1 in continental notation.

continuous blowdown valve

A device intended to reduce the number of BOILER washouts required by a STEAM LOCOMOTIVE. It worked by blowing a small but continuous stream of water out of the boiler while the REGULATOR was open.

continuous brakes (automatic)
The name given to any train braking system whereby all vehicles of a train are simultaneously braked when the system is operated by the guard or driver. The system will also be automatically applied in the event of the train being severed or any other aspect of the continuous braking suffering a failure. Since 1889, it has been a legal requirement to fit passenger trains with continuous automatic braking systems in the UK.

control orders
Orders from control which may concern most aspects of running the service including the arrangement of special trains, timetable and staff roster variations, allocation of work for locomotives and crews.

control trailer
An unmotored car housing the driving cab and controls of a multiple unit train. *See also* DIESEL MULTIPLE UNITS.

control, train or traffic
A system of organizing every aspect in the day to day running of a large, specifically defined area of railway from a central point by means of diagrams and telephones etc. The Midland Railway first introduced this system in 1907–12. Controllers would have wide powers over timetabling, staff and provision and organization of rolling stock movements, and would receive their information from various depots and signal boxes throughout their assigned territory.

controller (1)
One of the staff grades in the control method of operation.

controller (2)
The apparatus used to control motors of electric locomotives etc. It regulates the speed of the vehicles by varying the voltage and can also change direction of travel from forward to reverse.

convertible car
An early American tracer design which permitted the removal of its glass sides for summer working. It was particularly popular between 1890 and 1914.

Cook, Thomas (1808–1892)
The world-famous Thomas Cook organization was founded in 1841. Cook realized the potential of the railways for holiday travel. Aware of the overcrowding on most scheduled passenger trains, he organized an outing from Leicester to Loughborough (including tea and dancing) for some temperance workers. His idea soon caught on, and eventually expanded his horizons with 'Grand Tours' of Continental cities, and by the mid 1850s, Thomas Cook was one of the dominant names in world travel.

Copenhagen-Roskilde Railway
The Copenhagen-Roskilde was the first railway in what is now Denmark. It opened on 26 June 1847. Prior to this, the Altona-Kiel Railway had opened in 1844, but this was on territory which was subsequently annexed by Prussia.

Coronation
Between 1937 and 1939, the LONDON AND NORTH EASTERN RAILWAY operated the Coronation, a streamlined express featuring a 'beaver tail' observation car. For a supplementary fare, it offered meals at seats and a journey time of 6 hours from London to Glasgow.

Coronation Scot (1)
A streamlined express train operated by the LONDON MIDLAND

AND SCOTTISH RAILWAY between 1937 and 1939. It ran from London to Edinburgh in 6 hours and 30 minutes carrying a maximum of 232 passengers.

Coronation Scot (2)

The Coronation Scot, a streamlined Pacific designed by Sir William STANIER, achieved a British speed record of 114mph (183km/h) in 1937.

corridor

The passageway running along the side of compartment coaches to permit movement of passengers and staff throughout the train.

corridor tender

A special TENDER attached to a STEAM LOCOMOTIVE train which incorporated a side corridor to enable a crew change during long non-stop runs.

corrugation

Occasionally a regular pattern of hollows and ridges appears on the upper surface of rails, causing a roaring noise when a train passes over them. These corrugations appear for reasons not fully understood and are most often found on electric railways, but can be removed by rail-grinders.

cotter

The wedge used to tighten the ends of a STEAM LOCOMOTIVE's connecting rods.

couchettes

Low cost sleeping compartments used on French railways with double or triple berths.

country end

The term used to describe that end of a station which is opposite the London end.

coupé
The name given to a private compartment situated at the end of a luxury PULLMAN CAR; also the name for a half-compartment.

coupling rod
The rod visible on the exterior of a locomotive which couples the driving wheels together.

coupling screw
The two iron links which permit the couplings of fitted wagons and passenger wagons to be screwed tight in order to force the buffers together. This prevents high-speed oscillation.

cowcatcher
In the early days of rail travel in the United States, many of the early tracks lacked proper fences and consequently, animals were free to wander onto the lines. A collision with a large animal such as a buffalo could result in the derailment of a train, therefore cowcatchers were fitted to the front of the train to protect it. These large iron-barred structures simply swept away any offending animal, and gave American locomotives their distinctive appearance.

Crampton, Thomas Russell (1816–88)
Crampton was a locomotive and civil engineer who designed the famous single-driver locomotive, working alongside Daniel GOOCH at the GREAT WESTERN RAILWAY. The locomotive featured the situation of a large-diameter driving axle to the rear of the firebox, permitting a larger, low-pitched boiler. The first—the LIVERPOOL—was certainly speedy and apparently reliable, but it unfortunately destroyed the track and had to be scrapped in 1858. Perhaps because of this inauspicious start, British railway companies were reluctant to buy any future Cramptons, as they became known, with the exception of the South Eastern who were persuaded to take a batch. The French, however, were rap-

turous in their appreciation of the Crampton, and with a few modifications, Cramptons were soon running on the Nord, the Est and the PLM. The Crampton even enabled the Nord to become mainland Europe's fastest railways.

crossing
At a set of points or a DIAMOND CROSSING, the point upon which the wheels first touch the two lines of rail after one rail has crossed over another.

crossing place or loop
A section of double track provided on an otherwise single line to allow trains or trams travelling in the other direction to pass. These are usually situated at stations on a railway.

crossover/crossover road
A pair of rails connecting one line to another, to permit a train to change to the opposite direction of travel.

Croydon, Merstham and Godstone Railway
The Croydon, Merstham and Godstone Railway was incorporated on 17 May 1803. It opened on 24 July 1805, and ran from Croydon to Merstham.

culvert
A small pipe carrying water under a railway embankment.

Cunarder firsts
These were enormous first class coaches built for the boat trains which connected with Atlantic liners at Fishguard in West Wales between 1909 and 1914. Owned by GREAT WESTERN RAILWAY, they measured 21.34 metres (70 feet) in length and had eight compartments.

cut and cover
The method of tunnel building whereby a trench is cut out and

provided with a roof made from girders. The method was found to be too costly and disruptive for the building of underground railways. Sir Marc Brunel's (1769–1849) shield method was used in preference for the deeper tunnels required.

cut-off
Using the valve gear, the driver of a STEAM LOCOMOTIVE controlled the length of time for admission of steam to the CYLINDERS.

cylinders
The cylinder in a STEAM LOCOMOTIVE is basically a chamber which houses a piston. When the chamber is filled with steam, the piston is pushed back. Most cylinders permit the entry of steam from either side alternately, thus pushing the piston back and forth. The piston is attached to a driving wheel by means of a rod and crank. There are separate ports controlled by valves operating within a steam chest which allow for the entry of fresh steam and the exit of spent steam. Each time a cylinder piston moves back and forth, the rod and crank turn the driving wheel which completes one full rotation. The steam then leaves the cylinder and is exhausted to the atmosphere via the blastpipe and the chimney. Steam locomotives had either two, three or four cylinders, depending on their design.

D

damper
In order to regulate the air supply to the FIREBOX of a STEAM LOCOMOTIVE, the ash pan was fitted with a cover or damper.

danger ticket
A ticket collected by a driver from the signalman or pilotman in

control of a swing bridge. The train is not permitted to continue until the ticket has been collected by the signalman.

Danske Stadsbaner
Danish State railways.

dart
The catch located on the inside of the SMOKEBOX door in a STEAM LOCOMOTIVE.

dating press
The dating press was invented by Thomas Edmonson (1792–1851) in 1837 to stamp the issue date on cardboard passenger tickets. This device saved much labour involved in issuing tickets, previously been written by hand. His machine and system of storing numbered tickets on racks was in use on British railways for almost 150 years, right up until the late 1980s.

daylight sidings
Tracks for use only during daylight hours.

deadman's handle
The term describes the safety device in an electric train which is operated continuously by the driver (usually his foot) in order to prevent a break in the supply of current. In the event of the driver collapsing, and the pressure being lifted, the current is cut and the brakes applied. Also known as the driver's safety device, it was invented by J. F. Sprague in 1902.

Decapod
Any STEAM LOCOMOTIVE with 0–10–0 wheel arrangement.

Decauville track
Prefabricated track invented by Paul Amand Decauville for NARROW-GAUGE railways. Much used for French military railways, the 600mm gauge track came in unit lengths to allow for

easy transportation and rapid laying. The phrase 'Decauville track' or 'line' is now used to describe any light narrow gauge railway of 600mm gauge.

decklights
Long narrow windows situated in the clerestory or raised central roof section of a passenger coach.

deltics
Diesel-electric locomotives introduced in 1961 to BRITISH RAIL. These English Electric class 55, 3,300 horsepower locomotives were capable of 105mph (169 km/h).

demi-car
A small tramcar with a single deck designed for operation by one person.

detector bar
In signal interlocking, a detector bar will detect that the points are not properly home and alert the signalman (*see* SIGNALLING).

Deutsche Bahn
The name given to the new amalgamated German railway system (incorporating DEUTSCHE BUNDESBAHN and DEUTSCHE REICHSBAHN) following reunification in 1990.

Deutsche Bundesbahn
The Deutsche Bundesbahn was formed in 1949 to run those lines which had originally belonged to DEUTSCHE REICHSBAHN but lay in West Germany after the Federal Republic was created.

Deutsche Reichsbahn
The name given to the State German Railways, formed in 1923. Following the partition of Germany after the Second World War, the part of the system which remained in West Germany became DEUTSCHE BUNDESBAHN.

Deutsche Schlafwagen and Speiswagen Gesellschaft
The German Sleeping Car and Restaurant Car Company, which was formed in 1950 to run all such services on DEUTSCHE BUNDESBAHN. In 1990, the name changed to Deutsche Service Gesellschaft der Bahn.

diagram
A schedule made to provide the optimum working arrangements for crews and rolling stock for any given period. The diagram displays routes and services involved together with times.

diameter, wheel
The measurement of a train wheel's diameter is taken across the centre, omitting the FLANGE.

diamond crossing
A track which crosses another diagonally in such a way as to form a lozenge or diamond shape.

Diesel, Dr Rudolph (1858–1913)
Originally trained a regrigeration engineer, Rudolph Diesel achieved fame for his design of a compression ignition oil engine which took his name. It was, however, first invented by Herbert Stuart Akroyd (1864–1927) in 1890.

diesel-electric locomotives
A diesel-electric locomotive is in fact an electric locomotive that uses a diesel engine to power a generator which provides an electric current. The electricity produced then powers the motors which drive the wheels.

diesel-electric multiple units (DEMUs)
As with the DIESEL-ELECTRIC LOCOMOTIVE, the DEMU has a diesel engine which drives an electric generator which in turn powers traction motors which drive the wheels. Unlike DIESEL MULTIPLE UNITS, the combination of engine and generator is too large to be

positioned underfloor and is instead located in a power compartment to the rear of the driving cab. In one of the motorcoach's bogies are two traction motors which are supplied by electricity from the generator. Like the diesel multiple units, two or three units can be coupled and controlled either from a driving trailer or from the leading motorcoach. This type of vehicle has been largely withdrawn as a result of increasing electrification of lines, but the old Southern Region of BRITISH RAIL still operates a fleet on non-electrified lines.

diesel multiple units (DMUs)

Unlike a passenger train formed by coupling one locomotive to several coaches, a DMU consists of two to four vehicles, all with their own engines. These can all be coupled together and the engines are controlled from the one in front. The engines and transmissions are located under the floor to permit maximum space inside the coaches. Early DMUs could be comprised of various combinations of vehicles—for instance, coaches, driving trailers and trailers could all be included. The driving trailer would have a driver's compartment which also controlled the motorcoach when the driving trailer was leading. The second generation of DMUs in production since the 1980s have no drivers' compartments in intermediate motorcoaches although all vehicles are powered.

diesel power

Modern diesel engines are derived from Dr Rudolph DIESEL's basic design of 1897. Turbochargers are used to force air into the CYLINDERS where the rising pistons compress it and a temperature of around 980°C is achieved. As the piston reaches the top of the stroke, injectors pump a fine spray of oil into the cylinder where it is ignited by the heat. This causes expansion of the gases, which force the piston down. The pistons are connected to a crankshaft which operates the wheels, often through a system of gears. Most of British Rail's diesel engines operate a four-stroke cycle which operates as follows:

Stroke 1 Air is forced into the cylinder and the piston is pushed down. This turns the crankshaft.

Stroke 2 Oil is injected into the cylinder. The piston moves upwards raising the pressure in the cylinder and continuing to turn the crankshaft.

Stroke 3 The pressure heats the mixture until it is so hot that it explodes. The force of the explosion pushes the piston back down.

Stroke 4 The exhaust valve opens and the unused gas is released. The piston moves back up and the crankshaft has completed another turn.

diesel traction

Following some early experimental work with oil-fuelled locomotives in the 1870s and 80s in Russia and Britain, Rudolph DIESEL announced that his heavy-oil engine was the future of the railways. Further German development was temporarily halted by the First World War, but was continued by the Swedes who had the advantage of neutrality. Sweden's first diesel railcar went into service in 1913, and by 1920, eight were in operation. Its development really took off after the war at the hands of US, German and Soviet engineers who adapted it for a diversity of functions. Between 1928 and 1930, nearly 2000 diesel locomotives were built for shunting duties. In 1933, the FLYING HAMBURGER regularly reached 100mph (160km/h) in daily service.

At this time, a few experimental forays were made into the new technology in this country, but on the whole diesel was slow to catch on. The reason for this is likely to be the cost of oil in comparison with the low cost and high quality of coal readily available in this country. After the Second World War, this was no longer the case, and diesel oil became cheaper than coal.

diesel traction

Furthermore, high quality staff were easier to attract to diesel work, as it is much cleaner and easier to operate than steam. In terms of cost cutting, diesel has the advantage over steam in that it only needs one person to drive a locomotive.

Conversion was lamentably slow, in spite of the benefits which were evident from the experience of the US and other countries which were rapidly substituting steam for diesel. However, a few diesel locomotives were ordered and delivered for the LONDON, MIDLAND AND SCOTTISH RAILWAY in 1947, and the Southern Region of BRITISH RAIL took delivery of three between 1953 and 1954. Gradually, the BRITISH TRANSPORT COMMISSION awoke to the benefits of diesel traction and decided to invest substantially in its future. Although greater commitment was given to electrification in the Modernization Plan of 1955, it was realized that the benefits of diesel would be immediate and achievable at a lower capital outlay. In the years that followed, the design and building of diesel engines took off and emerged with a multitude of designs which reflected the still-experimental nature of the venture. Eventually, a few serviceable and reliable ranges of models remained. The most popular of these for passenger and freight work were the Peak class 44 and 45 which appeared in 1959. Later, class 47 were built in large numbers and were deployed in every part of the system, and after refitting, were still in use 20 years later for the fast trains operating between Edinburgh and Glasgow. Following the success of the class 47s, the only new engines required were for FREIGHT, and it was for this purpose that the class 58 Railfreight was introduced in 1982.

Demand for these passenger service locomotives had stagnated mainly due to the introduction of the High Speed Trains (HSTs), later known as INTERCITY 125S. These were introduced in 1976 and 1977. Powered by a diesel power-unit at each end, these trains ran regularly at speeds of up to 125mph (201km/h).

direttissima
Lines built by the Italian Ferrovia dello Stato to provide faster, more direct links between the larger Italian cities.

direttissimo
An Italian express train. Direttissimo were originally mail trains with restricted accommodation. **Diretto** is an ordinary express train, not as fast as a diretissimo.

disc
A ground signal.

display board
A white board mounted behind a SEMAPHORE signal to improve its visibility.

distant signal
The first signal seen by an oncoming train in a set of signals, usually situated a mile or three quarters of a mile in front of the first stop signal. If the stop (also known as home/outer home signal) is at danger, then distant signal will indicate the same. The driver will then reduce his speed until he can see the home signal. If the distant signal indicates 'off', it means that the next signal will also be 'off' or clear.

dock
A short dead-end length of track, often with a platform, built to accommodate coaches and other vehicles. Mostly used for loading and unloading FREIGHT. Dock was originally a canal term.

Dockland's Light Railway
The Docklands Light Railway in London was incorporated in 1984–5 and opened in 1987. It is remarkable in that it is the first computer-operated passenger railway in the UK to run driverless trains. This was the first line to open under the control of the new London Regional Transport.

double docking
The practice of permitting a second train into a terminal platform, thereby blocking the first's exit.

double shunt
The practice of using one uncoupled locomotive to shunt two sets of wagons to another line, when the sets are coupled together but are not coupled to each other.

double slips
A DIAMOND CROSSING which permits a train to proceed without crossing over the other line by means of connections in both directions between both tracks.

double-ended tank
Tank engine with symmetrical wheel arrangement, e.g. as 2-4-2T.

double-heading
Using two locomotives to haul one train.

down
The name given to describe the direction of travel either away from London, or wherever that particular railway's headquarters are located. In lines contained within Scotland, those running away from Edinburgh are described as down. The term is also applied to the train proceeding in that direction i.e. down train. This term originated in the days of road stagecoach travel.

down-siding
A SIDING coming off the down line.

drawbar
The hooked bar attached to the end frame of a rail vehicle to permit it to be coupled to others.

driver's safety device
See DEADMAN'S HANDLE.

driving trailer
A car with a cab installed, but without any traction equipment.

droplight
The part of the window in a coach door which can be raised and lowered and held in place with a leather strap in old vehicles or a spring clutch in more modern stock.

Dublin Area Rapid Transit
The electric rail service of Dublin and suburban area introduced in 1984.

Duchess
A Pacific-type (4–6–2) STEAM LOCOMOTIVE built for the LONDON MIDLAND AND SCOTTISH RAILWAY from 1937. It was designed by Sir William STANIER.

Duchess of Abercorn
STANIER'S non-streamlined Pacific No.6234 which, in 1939, achieved the incredible feat of hauling 610 tons up Beattock bank without falling below 31mph (50km/h). On the return journey, she reached Beattock summit at 60mph (97km/h), hauling the same load in the face of a howling blizzard at 60mph.

ducket
A small window at the side of a coach which is projected at an angle to permit the guard a clear view along the train and line.

Duke of Gloucester
Robert RIDDLES' No. 71000 Duke of Gloucester, a 'Britannia' type locomotive, has the sad distinction of being the last STEAM LOCOMOTIVE designed (1951) to run in Britain.

dumb buffer
A BUFFER which will not compress upon contact with another buffer.

dummy coach
A coach devoid of passengers sometimes coupled between locomotive and train for reasons of safety.

dumpling
A method of constructing tunnels under roads in which the side walls of the tunnel are constructed within two trenches excavated on both street sides. The road surface is then supported by timber baulks, then permanent steel girders are inserted. The earth (the dumpling) in the tunnel space is removed.

durchgangzuge/d-zuge
German fast corridor trains, often charging a supplementary fare.

dynamometer car
A special car coupled between the locomotive and the other vehicles of the train which is equipped with recording devices and instruments to measure the locomotives operating performance.

E

Eilzüge
Eilzüge or semi-fast trains running on the DEUTSCHE REICHSBAHN or the OSTERREICHISCHE BUNDESBAHN.

ears
The metal components into which trolley and suspension wires are soldered or clamped on a TRAMWAY.

Eason's specials
Between 1905 and 1939, J. W. Eason, a Grimsby travel agent, organized cheap excursion trains on the GNR and the LNR, using the slogan 'Good for the Public. Good for the Railway'.

East Coast main line
The railway which runs from London to Aberdeen via York, Newcastle, Edinburgh and Dundee.

East-West crossrail/crossrail
A main-line underground tube railway being built to connect ordinary trains with the underground system. The projected completion date is 1999 and it will run from Royal Oak to just east of Liverpool Street.

eastbound
(Also westbound etc.) From 1905, the London Underground Railways began to use these terms to describe a train heading in an easterly direction as opposed to the more traditional up and down.

Edinburgh and Glasgow railway
The Edinburgh and Glasgow Railway opened on 21 February 1842. It is one of the most level main-lines in the UK.

Edmonson ticket
The cardboard railway ticket, invented by Thomas Edmonson (1792–1851) which was used by British railways for almost 150 years, only being replaced by British Rail in 1989. The ticket was part of Edmonson's system which involved a dating press which numbered the tickets consecutively and printed upon them the date, the issuing station, the journey details and price. It can be found on some overseas railways, and on some preserved British railways. (*See also* DATING PRESS.)

ejector
A continuous jet of steam which keeps a STEAM LOCOMOTIVE's brakes off by maintaining a continuous vacuum.

electrification
In the 1820s, the English physicist Michael Faraday (1791–

1867) discovered that electricity could be used to create continuous motion, a discovery which initiated many attempts to power locomotives by this new method. Of the experiments that followed, that of German engineer Werner von SIEMENS, was the first which really alerted the railway world to the potential of electrification. Siemens' miniature engine successfully pulled three trucks carrying 30 passengers around a NARROW-GAUGE track at a speed of 4mph (6km/h), at the Berlin Exhibition of 1879.

By the time the world's first public railway opened at Lichterfelde near Berlin in 1881, Germany and America had already begun to adopt the safer option of electric power for engines working in mines. In 1883, Magnus VOLK layed a narrow gauge railway designed specifically for electric traction on the Brighton foreshore which still runs today. Volk's engine ran on a very low voltage, but it was quickly realized that if long distance rail travel by this method were to become a reality, a higher voltage was required.

The Brighton railway generated its own current, but by the 1880s, higher voltage power was just beginning to become available via coal-fired or water driven generating plants, such as the hydro-electric generating plant in Wisconsin which opened in 1882. However, it took some years before it became possible to transmit the power generated by these new power stations over any significant distance. Once available, the inexorable drive to electrify railways had begun.

The American Charles Van Depoele is generally credited as being the first to perfect the use of overhead electric transmission with the development of a trolley which travelled along a conductor arm mounted on the roof collecting current. (It was considered too dangerous to electrify the track itself.) Another American, F. J. SPRAGUE, devised a method of fitting electric motors to existing BOGIES on the New York Elevated Railway

electrification

cars. He later developed a method of controlling the current of several coupled vehicles from the leading car.

In Britain, the success of the Brighton railway together with the continuing improvements in the supply had been very encouraging, and the engineers on the new tube railway which was under construction in London (the City and South London) decided that it should be powered by electricity. In 1893, the Liverpool Overhead Railway came into operation using electricity. It was used primarily by dock workers, but it was unable to compete with trams and motor buses and was eventually closed in 1956 as it was running at a loss. However, it maintains its place in history as the first electrically powered elevated railway in the world.

Otherwise, electrification was proving a huge success. Between 1898 and 1907, more electrified tube railways were opened in London, and the tube system as we know it now began to emerge. Gradually, the railway companies were alerted to the benefits of electrification in terms of speed and cleanliness, particularly on suburban lines. Unfortunately, at least eight different systems were in use, with railways free to select whichever they preferred. Eventually, in 1951, the British Transport Commission issued its first directive requiring that all future electrification should be of the same 1,500 volt DC system with a few exceptions which allowed for future development.

Widespread electrification was provided for in the nationalized British Railways Modernization Plan of 1955. A 25,000 volt alternating current via overhead wires was adopted, with the exception of the Southern Region. By 1974, most of the West Coast main line from London to Glasgow had been electrified, and the East Coast main line between London, Peterborough, Doncaster, York, Newcastle and Edinburgh was completely electrified in 1991.

In the course of main-line electrification between 1967 and

1974, a new class of electric locomotive was called for. Up until 1967, the use of electric locomotives had not been widespread, although some lines had been using a few since the early years of the century. The Metropolitan Railway had run a small fleet of electric locomotives to the boundaries of that part of its operations which had electrified lines since 1907. These were completely rebuilt in 1922 and continued in service until 1961. The LONDON AND NORTH EASTERN RAILWAY also built electric locomotives (mainly for freight) and indeed lent some of them to the Netherlands after the second World War where they were known as Tommies. In 1967, British Railways developed some 200 class 81–87 electric locomotives which ran mainly between Euston and Birmingham, and Manchester, Liverpool and Glasgow averaging 70–75mph (112–120km/h).

The Advanced Passenger Train (APT) was designed to reach much higher speeds than this on existing tracks. It incorporated a revolutionary tilting mechanism to allow it to negotiate bends at speed. However, it was destined to spend only two weeks in service in 1981, dogged with technical problems. More success has been achieved with the Class 91 GEC design electric locomotive (sometimes known as the InterCity 225) with its top speed of 140mph (225km/h).

In Britain's 25kV ac electrified lines, power comes from the national grid to feeder stations which transform the current to 25kV. It then travels through circuit breakers to the overhead wires which can be seen above the track. The passing train then collects the current via a pantograph or 'arm'.

electroten
A fast Spanish electric train.

electroteni
The fastest Italian electric trains, usually First Class and charging a supplementary fare.

elevated railway

A rapid transit urban passenger railway which runs on steel structures above the city streets.

Empresa de los Ferrocarriles del Estado

Chilean State Railways.

English Electric

English Electric is a company formed in 1918–19 by the merging of Dick, Kerr and Co. Ltd, Phoenix Dynamo Manufacturing Co. Ltd. and Willans Robinson. In 1968, English Electric was absorbed into GEC. English Electric supplied not only electric and DIESEL LOCOMOTIVES and railcars, buses, tram and trolleycars, but also large generating plant and switchgear and radio valves.

excursion trains

Until the late 1960s and early 1970s, BRITISH RAIL occasionally ran passengers trains (usually consisting of old rolling stock) subject to various special conditions (such as prohibition of luggage) for much reduced fares. The idea was probably Thomas COOK'S, who ran excursion trains for workers as early as 1841. Such excursion trains were often known as 'Half-day', 'Day' and 'Evening'. The term 'excursion' is also used for cheap tickets on selected regular trains using normal rolling stock or for trains chartered by private parties.

exhibition train

A train which tours around the country displaying new equipment or services.

expreso

A Spanish express train.

express freight

A FREIGHT system operated only in North America in which private freight companies took responsibility for luggage and freight consignments. Fast passenger trains were used to transport the freight and the company would arrange for its collection and distribution at the journey's end. The system was first used in 1839, and the best-known of the express freight companies were American Express and Wells Fargo.

F

face
The name given to the part of a platform next to the track.

facing point detector
A device preventing the relevant signal being moved to 'off' before full completion of the point movement.

facing point locks
These bolts secure the points which must be run over in the direction facing in order that the route or train signal can be moved to indicate 'off'.

facing points
The points which offer a choice of route and which face the train's direction of travel.

facing points bar
A bar designed to stop any movement of facing points as a train passes over them.

Fairlie
An articulated STEAM LOCOMOTIVE invented in 1863 and which took the name of its inventor, Robert Francis Fairlie.

fall-plate
A hinged steel plate which covers the gap between locomotive

and TENDER. The name is also given to a steel plate situated between two coaches with open-ended balconies.

fang bolt
A bolt screwed through a flat-bottomed rail's lower FLANGE and is held by a nut onto the SLEEPER.

fang spike
The metal spike used to secure a flat-bottomed rail to the SLEEPER.

feed pipe
The pipe which supplies water to the BOILER of a steam locomotive from the tank or TENDER.

feed-water heater
A device which heats water prior to its entry to the BOILER of a STEAM LOCOMOTIVE.

Ferrocarriles Argentinos
Argentinian State Railways.

Ferrovie Dello Stato/FS
Italian State Railways.

Ffestiniog Railway
The Ffestiniog Railway opened in 1836 to carry slate traffic. Initially, it opened as a NARROW-GAUGE (597mm) horseway, but in the 1860s the engineer Charles Spooner had proper railway tracks laid. In 1863, the Ffestiniog became the world's first narrow-gauge railway to have steam traction. Until 1864, it hauled only slate from Blaenau-Ffestiniog to Portmadog, then the Board of Trade granted it a licence to run a passenger service. In 1865, the Ffestiniog became the first ever narrow-gauge railway to carry passengers. Since 1954, the Ffestiniog has operated as a preserved private tourist railway (*see* page 179 for details).

firebox
The firebox is that section of a steam locomotive situated just in front of the cab and containing the coal fire, comprised of an outer and an inner firebox. The inner firebox had a firegrate and dampers which controls fuel combustion. The firebox has an arch of firebrick, known as the brick arch, which deflects the hot gases of the fire and directs them evenly along the flue tubes.

fireman
In the age of steam locomotion, the crew usually consisted of two people, a driver and a fireman. The fireman's duties were to stoke the fire to ensure a plentiful steam supply, and to keep a check on the BOILER's water level by observing gauge glass indicators in the cab. When the water level fell, he would fill the boiler by operating the injector control. He also helped the driver to read signals, especially on curved sections of track.

fishplates
The metal plate used to secure rail joints and to reinforce them, so-called because the original plates resembled a fish shape when the two halves were fitted together. Fishplates were invented by William Bridges ADAMS who patented them in 1847.

fitted freight or goods
The name given to a FREIGHT train fitted with CONTINUOUS BRAKES.

fixed distance
A distant signal which is unworked and left permanently in the 'on' position, to indicate a speed restriction or passing loop or an approach to a passenger platform.

flagging
The control of train movements by green and red flags at times of signal breakdown or track repair. *See also* SIGNALLING.

flagman
The rail employee who operates the green and red flags at times of signal failure etc. *See also* SIGNALLING.

flaman
A speedometer and speed recording device which are compulsory on FRENCH RAILWAYS.

flange
The 25mm lip that extends from the inner rim of the train wheel. The flange guides the wheels of the train along the tracks.

flange lubricators
Lubricating devices situated on the rails which lubricate wheel flanges on curved sections of track with the purpose of reducing excess rail wear.

flat bottom rail
A rail which is flat at the bottom to enable it to be fixed directly to the SLEEPER.

flighting
The name given to the operational tactic of running groups of trains travelling at similar speeds to achieve optimum line capacity.

Flying Hamburger/Fliegende Hamburger
A two-car diesel-electric articulated streamlined locomotive introduced by the DEUTSCHE REICHSBAHN in the spring of 1933. At that time it was the world's fastest train, running Europe's first 100mph (161km/h) passenger service.

Flying Scotsman
The Flying Scotsman became one of the world's most famous STEAM LOCOMOTIVES when it achieved the first British official 100mph (161km/h) on rail in 1934. Designed by Sir Herbert GRESLEY, the Flying Scotsman was the first steam train to com-

plete the 392 miles (631km) journey from London to Edinburgh non-stop. This feat, which it managed regularly in summertime, has never been surpassed by a steam engine.

fog detonator
Disc-shaped detonators which are clipped to the rail surface in pairs to warn drivers of obstructions up ahead or of signals invisible as a result of fog.

fogging machine
A device which places and removes detonators on the line to coincide with 'on' and 'off' signals.

fog gongs
Electric gongs used on signals in foggy conditions to warn drivers of their locations and to prevent the over-running of trains in the event of the 'on' indication.

fogmen
Railway employees who place FOG DETONATORS on the tracks and signal trains by means of flags and lamps when semaphore signals are rendered invisible by fog.

fog pit
A pit situated between the rails which permit FOGMEN to attach detonators to the line.

fog repeater
During periods of reduced visibility, a colour-light signal is used to repeat the normal signal ahead in advance.

formation
The term used to describe either the track bed and earthworks of a railway or the composition of a train.

Forth Bridge Railway
The Forth Bridge Railway was opened in 1890 and operated ini-

tially by the North British Railway. It was later taken over by the London and North Eastern Railway in 1923, until becoming part of the nationalized British Rail network in 1948.

fouling bar
A bar connected to the signals located on the trackside which prevents signals being switched to 'off' when the weight of a train depresses it.

fouling point
The point where tracks converge beyond which a vehicle would obstruct another attempting to pass.

fourth class
A fourth (and not surprisingly inferior) passenger class was introduced on some services run by the Manchester and Leeds Railway, the Edinburgh and Glasgow Railway and the Great Northern Railway in the 1840s–50s. However, it was withdrawn after only a few years, although a cheap fourth class with few seats continued to operate in Europe into the 20th century. Such a service continued in Germany until 1928.

Fowler's Ghost
This was the nickname given to Sir John Fowler's prototype steam locomotive the design of which was intended to minimize steam and smoke emissions in the tunnels of the Metropolitan Railway. The engine was built by Stephenson & Co. in 1861, but was not a success.

Fowler, Sir John (1817–1898)
A civil engineer best known for his work on the Inner Circle of the Metropolitan Railway in London. Together with Benjamin Baker, he was assigned with the construction on the Forth Railway Bridge. The bridge took over seven years to build, costing £3,000,000 and the lives of 56 men.

frame, mechanical
The apparatus which usually housed the levers and interlocking for manually operated signals and points. The equipment was usually located in a signalbox, or occasionally on a station platform.

Franco-Crosti boiler
A boiler designed by A. Franco in Belgium and later improved upon by Piero Crosti. The system allowed the feed water for the boiler to be heated by exhaust fumes in a secondary drum to a temperature almost as high as that achieved in the boiler, thereby increasing efficiency. First built in Belgium in 1932, improved versions were produced in Italy in 1940. In 1955, BRITISH RAIL had ten locomotives incorporating Franco-Crosti boilers.

free trucking
A service providing free transportation of theatrical equipment for touring companies using the railways. The service was withdrawn in 1964.

freight
The name used for all non-passenger railway traffic. It was originally an American term, but came into general railway usage after the 1900s.

freight trains
From the earliest days of the railways, the need to carry goods has been a driving force in their development. The early freight trains would consist of two or three horse-drawn wagons, normally carrying coal or mineral ore. With the advent of steam, it was possible to operate longer trains at higher speeds, although early brake systems restricted the maximum speed of a fully loaded locomotive.

Early freight locomotives were coupled to wagons which were

freight trains

usually unconnected to its brakes. To slow the train, the driver would operate the brake in the locomotive and the guard would operate the brake on one of the vans—the brake van. The perilous braking mechanism restricted freight trains to a speed of 30mph (48km/h). Nowadays, continuous brakes mean that the brake van has disappeared.

Until the Transport Act of 1968, the railways were COMMON CARRIERS which meant that they had a duty to accept carriage of any goods presented to them. This worked well for the railways in the early days, when their only real competitors were the canal and waterway operators, but increasing road transport meant that the railways lost many of the smaller, easily transported goods. Once many of the railways' customers had deserted them, they were mainly left with large and awkward loads, and the provision of a general freight service became unsustainable. After 1968, the National Freight corporation took over the conveyance of small consignments, often using road vehicles which had once belonged to the railways.

BRITISH RAIL then set up Speedlink, a wagonload service consisting of 75mph (120km/h) trains with air-braked wagons. This had the advantage that for customers with regular heavy loads, it could often travel to railway depots from customers' private sidings. However, in the long run, the service proved uneconomic and was discontinued in 1990.

Nowadays, British Rail mainly operates freight in trainloads, i.e. each train carries a particular type of freight. The greatest innovations, however, are seen in international freight transport now that a rail link with Europe has been established via the CHANNEL TUNNEL. Intermodal transport, first tried in the UK in the 1950s, involves transferring road trailers or vehicle bodies to rail wagons. One example of this is the 'Piggyback' system, in which the entire truck and cab are transferred to a wagon. Unfortunately, British LOADING GAUGE prohibits this in much of mainland Britain, but since 1991, a few such services have been provided. Another system uses special trailers which are adapted to run on road or rail. Possibly the best-known intermodal system in this country is the Freightliner service, which carried container loads on special wagons known as container flats.

French railways

Surprisingly, France was relatively slow to join the great wave of railway building in the 19th century, possibly because of its predominantly agricultural economy and also because there was in existence a fairly good system of roads. Many government critics were urging greater industrialization, and improvement in the transport system, which naturally meant rail. After much indecision and deliberation on the government's part on whether or not any system should be state or privately funded, the Pereire brothers finally succeeded in obtaining a franchise to operate a passenger service from Le Pecq to the Pont L'Europe and Rue Saint-Lazare. It enjoyed phenomenal success, and was instantly patronized by enthusiastic Parisians who travelled on hourly trains which ran from 7am until 10pm.

It was decided following the collapse of the Paris–Orléans company in 1840, that the development of a first rate railway system was too important to be left to the vagaries of private enterprise. In 1842, the Assembly laid the foundations for a rational system of state-run trunk lines. Great vision coupled with a disregard for civil engineering cost meant that France was provided with the basis of the much envied high-speed system which exists today. Private companies were still responsible for laying track, providing rolling stock and buildings, and manning and running the railways, but the State and the individual local authorities provided earthworks, trackbeds and engineering structures. In return, the State retained some control over

French railways

the overall shape of the industry and the companies' spheres of influence. Perhaps most importantly, the 1842 law provided for future State repurchase of the entire new system, if necessary.

Great progress was made in the railway-building programme until the revolution of 1848, which had targeted the railways on account of their use of foreign contractors, workers and engineers. (Indeed, many of these were British, as French expertise was still at an early stage in its development.) As a result of loss of business and physical damage to many lines at this time, many companies ceased to operate and either sold out to bigger concerns or were taken over by the state.

At the time of Napoleon III's second empire, 77 companies of various sizes existed. Napoleon himself supported and encouraged mergers—with great success—so that by 1858, the 77 companies had merged and reformed into six. These were the Nord, the Est, the Paris-Orléans, the Midi, the Ouest and the Paris-Lyon Méditerranée. These were all granted 99 year leases as part of a contract signed by the Ministry of Works which laid down detailed specifications governing the running of the service in its Cahiers de Charges.

The Franco-Prussian War (1870–1) heralded a new crisis for French railways, which were held partly to blame for France's defeat. The Est line had suffered much damage on the front line, and elsewhere routine maintenance had lapsed. Some of the smaller railways had fallen into the hands of a Belgian banker by the name of Philippart, whose financial empire collapsed in 1877. The state rescued them and regrouped them as the Etat railway, which in due course absorbed the flagging Ouest railway. Under the engineer Louis de Saulces de Freycinet, a new boom in French railway building was triggered.

De Freycinet envisaged a gradual nationalization of the railway system, but as chief of the Ministry of Public works he undertook to provide every provincial town of prefecture or subprefecture status with a standard gauge line. Although the Freycinet plan was well enough intentioned, its effect was to furnish France with a ridiculous surfeit of rural lines, notwithstanding that it ultimately fell short of providing sub-prefectures with rail transport.

The French railway system was finally nationalized on 1 January 1938, and the principal railways were nationalized to form the Société Nationale de Chemins de fer Français known as SNCF. In a decree of 1937, the SNCF was empowered to operate the railways until 31 December 1982. In 1983, its legal status was re-established and a new decree was issued on 18 February 1983. It provided for even greater commitment to improving standards and securing new customers, and also for overhaul and modifications to its financial structure and executive council, with the eventual aim of becoming financially solvent.

full and standing
The official term for a train which is well loaded.

fully fitted train
A train fitted with CONTINUOUS BRAKES and upon which at least 90% of the vehicles have continuous brakes.

funnel
Another term for the chimney of a STEAM LOCOMOTIVE, adopted by GREAT WESTERN RAILWAY for a time.

G

de Glehn, Alfred George (1848–1936)
De Glehn was a French pioneer of locomotive compounding. His COMPOUND STEAM ENGINES enjoyed great success with the

Nord railway company in France and were soon in great demand in Prussia, Egypt and India. From 1910 onwards, de Glehn's compound engines were superheated which was probably the most important contributory factor to their undisputed prowess. G. J. CHURCHWARD was so impressed by these engines that he ordered three de Glehn ATLANTICS for GREAT WESTERN RAILWAY, although he finally abandoned compound engines altogether.

gallery
The term given to the gantry housing the signals and also the upper deck of a double–decker suburban train.

gangway
The metal plate providing access between a STEAM LOCOMOTIVE and its TENDER or between coaches. A coach fitted with a gangway (or FALL PLATE) is described as 'gangwayed'.

Garrat, Herbert William (1864–1913)
Garratt invented an articulated steam locomotive with an engine at each end, linked by a frame carrying the BOILER. Beyer-Peacock built two of these compound engines for Tasmania, and a simple expansion version of these early Garratts went on to power many of the railways in South Africa. Many railways around the world took delivery of Garratts, particularly those of NARROW GAUGE.

gate box
A signal box with the specific purpose of controlling level crossings.

gauge
The GAUGE or distance between rails been set at about 1435mm (4ft 8in) since Roman times. Although it is uncertain as to why this seemingly arbitrary figure was chosen, it may be that the

grooves created between the stone slabs used to pave Roman streets were about this distance apart and provided a natural tramway for wagons and chariots. Another theory suggests that a wagon measuring 1435mm in width may have been the widest that a single colliery worker could push in pre-mechanization times. However, 1435mm was the gauge favoured by George STEPHENSON for the STOCKTON AND DARLINGTON RAILWAY, later widening to allow for FLANGED wheels.

The standard gauge was established at 1435mm in this country and many others (BRITISH RAIL later modified this to 1432mm to limit lateral oscillation on BOGIES), although it was subject to criticism from many quarters in the early days of steam locomotion. Clearly the size of the locomotive would be dictated by the size of the gauge, and some eminent critics (including BRUNEL) felt that a wider gauge would allow a larger, faster and more stable engine with a lower centre of gravity. Brunel's challenge to the STEPHENSONS was to build a line with a massive 2438mm (7ft) gauge for the GREAT WESTERN RAILWAY, which did in fact set records for speed which remained unbroken for many years. In Britain, there gradually came to exist a multiplicity of gauges—no fewer than six varying between 1371mm in Scotland to GWR's 2438mm.

Eventually, the government was forced to take action and the Gauge Act was passed in 1846 outlawing the building of any new track which was not of the standard 1435mm. The Great Western Railway was permitted to continue with projected plans for BROAD-GAUGE extensions on the condition that it adapt existing track to mixed gauge by adding a third rail at its own expense.

In the event, the Great Western Railway was eventually forced to reduce its gauge to 1524mm due to difficulties incurred in the movements of goods as a result of its neighbours' smaller gauges.

gauge glass
A tube located in the cab which displays the level of water in the BOILER. A similar gauge also exists to display the height of the water in the TENDER.

gauntletted track
Gauntletted track is where two sets of parallel tracks are arranged with the inner rail of one set between the other set. Gauntletted track is generally used on viaducts or tunnels under repair to permit extra working space. Thereafter, that gauntletted section can only be operated and signalled as single track.

German railways
The first railway to be built in Germany was the Nürnberg to Fürth line which opened on 7 December 1835. It was known as the Ludwigsbahn after Ludwig I of Bavaria who authorized its construction. The Ludwigsbahn's first steam locomotive was Der Adler, designed by Robert STEPHENSON. In its first year, the LUDWIGSBAHN enjoyed astonishing success, carrying over 450,000 passengers, and alerted commercial enterprise to the possibilities of rail transport.

At this time, Germany consisted of many diverse grand duchies and kingdoms. However, by 1850, Germany already boasted more than 3276 miles (6000km) of railway, with plans for many more underway. In fact, several of the eight main state railways which were eventually to form the Reichsbahn were already in existence: Hanover, Baden, Bavaria Württemberg and Prussia. With the unification of Germany in 1871, the individual state railways were nationalized, and finally united in 1919 under the Weimar Constitution. The German State Railway (DEUTSCHE REICHSBAHN) was established by the Railway Act of 1924. Following the Second World War, Germany was partitioned and those railways which lay in the Communist East continued as Deutsche Reichsbahn (DR). The Western portion of the railway became the DEUTSCHE BUNDESBAHN of German Federal Railway (DB).

German reunification in 1990 has necessitated further reorganization. The two systems have been re-united to form a new company, Deutsche Bahn AG, which has been in operation since January 1994.

Gladstone, William Ewart (1809–1898)
In 1844, during Gladstone's secong term as Liberal prime minister, the great railway mania was at its height in Britain. Gladstone's parliament passed an act that year that gave government the authority to purchase any new railway company at any time after 21 years had elapsed, and attempted to provide for the reasonable comfort and safety of third class passengers. The original bill for the act had intended to give the government even greater control over the running and management of the railway companies, but vested interest ensured that this did not appear in the final act which was in any event modified to affect only new companies. However, although the purchasing powers of the act were never actually used at the time, its main success was that it had laid down a principle which was to exert a profound influence at the time of railway NATIONALIZATION in 1947.

Golsdorf, Dr Karl (1861–1916)
Dr Golsdorf was appointed chief locomotive engineer to Austrian State Railways in 1891. He developed Anatole MALLET's COMPOUND ENGINE principles and produced around sixty classes of locomotive capable of negotiating the varied and often hazardous routes of Austria.

Gooch, Sir Daniel (1816–1889)
In 1837, Daniel Gooch, an engineer, was appointed locomotive superintendent on the GREAT WESTERN RAILWAY at the age of 21, beginning what was to be a highly successful partnership with

another innovative young engineer, Isambard Kingdom BRUNEL. Gooch established the GREAT WESTERN RAILWAY locomotive works in 1840. He resigned from the Great Western Railway in 1864, but returned as chairman in 1865 at a time when the company was foundering and restored it to its former success. He was also responsible for the laying of the first transAtlantic cable, for which he was knighted.

Grand Junction Railway
The Grand Junction opened between Birmingham and Warrington on the 4 July 1837, connecting the Liverpool and Manchester with the London and Birmingham. Later, it became a section of the main London to Glasgow line.

Greathead, James Henry (1844–96)
Greathead was born in South Africa but moved to England in 1858 to study civil engineering. In 1869 he undertook work to build a subway beneath the Thames in London. At this time he devised the Greathead shield, a cyliner-shaped tube propelled by screws for use in tunnelling the London Underground system. By 1884 the shield had been improved to use compressed air and hydraulic jacks to produce forward propulsion.

Great Western
An engine designed by Daniel GOOCH in 1846 for the GREAT WESTERN RAILWAY. It was similar in design to the PATENTEE but has the distinction of being the first engine to be built at the Great Western Railway's Swindon workshops. Along with the IRON DUKE, the Great Western was the first engine to consistently haul loads at over 60mph (96.5km/h)

Great Western Railway
The Great Western Railway opened on 4 June 1838, with its first section from Paddington to Maidenhead. It became famous for its broad gauge of 2438mm and the engineers who worked

on it—most notably Isambard Kingdom BRUNEL and Daniel GOOCH. Brunel always insisted upon the broad gauge, maintaining that it was the optimum width to permit a locomotive built to travel at speed without jeopardizing stability. Certainly, GWR's locomotives, designed by Gooch at the company's Swindon works, were for many years unrivalled for speed and comfort. However, because most other railway companies had opted for the standard gauge of 1435mm, freight customers using the GWR frequently suffered long delays and loss of freight wherever a break in gauge necessitated its transfer to another train. Eventually the GWR was compelled to convert to standard gauge, and its broad-gauge trains ceased to run on 20 May 1892.

Gresley, Sir Herbert Nigel (1876–1941)
Gresley trained as a mechanical engineer in the London and North Railway (Crewe) and the Lancashire and Yorkshire Railway (Harwich). In 1905, he was appointed Wagon and Carriage superintendent of the Great Northern Railway, and succeeded Ivatt as chief mechanical engineer six years later. He produced class after class of locomotives which were to prove reliable and durable. The most famous of these was the A4 class of PACIFIC of which No. 4468 MALLARD broke the world speed record for a steam locomotive. It reached 126mph (203km/h), a record which remains the fastest speed recorded by a steam engine.

H

Hackworth, Timothy (1786–1850)
Timothy Hackworth worked with William HEDLEY as foreman/smith at the time PUFFING BILLY was built at Wylam. As resident

engineer/manager on the Stockton and Darlington Railway, he designed the Royal George, the first six-coupled locomotive on which the cylinders drove onto the wheels directly. With his engine the Sans Pareil, he entered the famous RAINHILL TRIALS, but was forced to withdraw when the cylinder cracked. A second Sans Pareil, however, went on to serve the York, Newcastle and Berwick Railway successfully until 1881.

hanging buffers
Wooden vertical buffers which allow a wagon to be coupled with a wagon with lower-level buffers.

Hawkshaw, Sir John (1811–91)
Sir John Hawkshaw was the civil engineer who was responsible for the laying of some of the most difficult lines in the Pennines for the Lancashire and Yorkshire Railway. He was later engineer on the East London Railway, but is best known for the Severn Tunnel, which was completed in 1887.

Hedley, William (1779–1843)
Hedley was colliery manager at Wylam when he decided to try out an experiment on his employer's newly acquired cast-iron plate rails. (The owner of the colliery, Captain Blackett had declined the opportunity to run a STEAM LOCOMOTIVE on Wylam Railway as the existing wooden tracks could not withstand the weight of the engine.) He designed a carriage with handles attached to each of the four wheels and provided footboards upon which men could stand in order to turn the handles and propel the carriage along the tracks. Once he had ascertained the optimum weight of the motive power required to propel the engine along smooth wheels and tracks, he mounted an engine on his carriage. The system worked well, but as he had not used the return flue type designed by Richard TREVITHICK, the engine was frequently short of steam. However, Hedley had confirmed that

John BLENKINSOP's toothed wheel and rack system was unnecessary. He also discovered that adhesion could be enhanced by applying the use of gears to more than one set of wheels. In fact, it is likely that the general appearance of Hedley's engine was rather similar to that of Trevithick's.

Spurred on by his early success, Hedley began to build locomotives to his own design. The first in 1813, was followed by a second in 1814, both of which ran at Wylam with some success. It became evident that plate rails were unable to cope with the load, a problem which Hedley overcame by mounting his engines on eight wheels. The engines worked well until the plate rails were superseded by edge rails, which necessitated a return to the original four-wheel design. This time, however, the wheels were flanged. Although much rebuilt and modified during their working lives, these locomotives—the famous PUFFING BILLY which can still be seen at the Royal Science Museum in London, and Wylam Dilly on display at the Royal Museum of Scotland in Edinburgh.

Holden, James (1837–1925)

In the twelve years he was employed as locomotive engineer for the Great Eastern Railway, James Holden designed no less than eleven classes of simple, reliable and economic locomotives, the best known of which were the Claud Hamilton class of 1900. He also produced a huge 0–10–0 tank engine in 1902 to fend off the electrification lobby. The Decapod as it was known, demonstrated that it could travel from 0–30mph (0–48km/h) in 30 seconds—the claim which was being made for electric locomotives. This set back any electrification programme the Great Eastern Railway might have considered, despite the fact that the *Decapod* was too large and ungainly to be used on a regular basis.

Hudson, George (1800–71)

George Hudson was Britain's first railway tycoon. A draper of

York, who later became Lord Mayor, a Tory MP and self-styled 'King of the Railways', Hudson had achieved control of nearly half of England's huge railway network by the time he was 46 years old. At the time of the great railway-building mania, Hudson had no interest in railways other than as a money-making proposition. He achieved an initial illusion of profit by means of paying low wages and skimping on materials. Thereafter, he succeeded in blackmailing and bullying numerous companies into coming under his control. This achieved, he used capital from these companies to pay dividends to shareholders. His eventual and inevitable demise revealed a catalogue of fraud and illicit share dealing.

I

Indian railways

Although India was undoubtedly the jewel in the British colonial crown, railway development gained momentum very slowly. Commercial enterprise in India was largely controlled by the ineffectual East India Company, whose directors had little interest in railways. Eventually John Chapman, an entrepreneur, put forward a very well-reasoned case for Indian railway development, and succeeded in wheedling some capital from the East India Company. Chapman received authorization for the building of his Great Indian Peninsular Railway (GIP) and East Indian Railway in 1848. More auspicious still was the arrival in that same year of the New Governor General of India, Sir James Dalhousie.

Sir James's experience on the British Board of Trade had made him a staunch advocate of the railways. He enthusiastically set about enabling the construction of a comprehensive network of railways to connect the main ports with the interior, and stimulated British investment in his scheme by securing a Government guarantee of a dividend of not less than 5%. In return, the government could take over the railway after a period of 25 years had elapsed. Furthermore, the government was to decide on the routes and all railway building had to comply with government standards.

The net effect of the so-called Dalhousie minute was that India was provided with the most rationally planned system in Asia. Construction standards were also high, and soaring civil engineering costs resulted in the loss of vast amounts of money by the end of the 1860s. At this point the government took over railway construction, but had little more success in curbing costs and returned the responsibility to private enterprise once more.

Despite passionate pleas on the part of the engineer Guilford Molesworth not to proceed, the government embarked on a programme of NARROW-GAUGE lines (the Indian standard gauge was 1676mm) mainly in more remote areas. Molesworth was vindicated, as the lines were never a commercial success as a result of constant breaks in gauge hindering the passage of freight.

Before the partition of India in 1947, Indian Railways comprised a total of 18,628 miles (29,997km) of standard 1676mm gauge, 14,150 miles (22,786km) of 1000mm gauge and 1960 miles (3157km) of 610mm gauge, shared between ten main and 78 smaller railways. When India was partitioned and Pakistan created, many of the lines of the North West and Bengal and Assam systems were truncated at frontiers and many costly new connecting lines had to be constructed as old through routes were torn apart. In 1950, the entire railway system became unified (excepting Pakistan) as Indian (Government) Railways. Today, the total route length is around 38,572 miles (62,113km), still on varying gauges, with 4538 miles (7308km) of 1676mm track and 103 miles (166km) of 1000mm track electrified.

InterCity 125 diesel train (IC 125)

The InterCity 125 consists of between seven and nine trailers with a Class 43 High Speed Power Train at each end. These locomotives were built between 1976 and 1982 by BREL Crewe Works. These still work on main lines which have yet to be electrified and travel at speeds of up to 125mph (201km/h). They are also still used on various lines out of King's Cross which are initially electrified but have destinations outwith the electrified system. Control wires run the length of the train between power cars in order that one cab can control both of the engine generator sets.

Irish Railways

The first Irish railway opened on 17 December 1834 and ran between Dublin and Dun Laoghaire (at that time known as Kingstown). Originally built to standard 1435mm gauge, it was later converted in 1857 to the Irish standard gauge of 1600mm. Today, Ireland has 1209 miles (1947km) of 1600mm track.

Iron Duke

The Iron Duke locomotive was designed by DANIEL GOOCH for the BROAD-GAUGE GREAT WESTERN RAILWAY along the lines of the PATENTEE. Built in 1846, it consistently pulled loads at over 60mph (97km/h).

Italian Railways

The first Italian railway opened in 1839 and ran from Naples to Portici, but further railway development was greatly hampered by political instability, and by 1848 only a handful of lines were in existence. When Italian unification finally came in 1862, the new government of the Kingdom of Italy were quick to realize that the railways were an essential part of integration. Spurred on by an offer from the state to reimburse all construction costs, companies began constructing a system in earnest, and within four years, most of the major cities were connected, with the exception of the deprived South.

In 1865, the government ordered that the various companies be grouped into four, a step which was to facilitate nationalization in 1905. At this time, all the major lines were incorporated into a government department, the Ferrovie dello Stato (FS). FS became an independent state-owned corporation in 1986, until December 1992, when it was transformed into the joint-stock company FS SpA, whose entire share capital is held by the treasury.

Today, FS SpA boasts 9976 miles (15,961km) of 1435mm track. Of this, 6685 miles (10,764 km) is electrified.

Ivatt, Henry Alfred (1851–1923)
Ivatt spent ten years as a locomotive engineer on the Great Southern and Western Railway in Ireland, until his appointment as chief mechanical engineer at the Great Northern Railway, Doncaster. He was the first to introduce an ATLANTIC (4–4–2) type locomotive to Britain. Upon his retirement in 1911, he was succeeded by GRESLEY.

J

Japanese railways
The return to power of the Emperor in 1867 resulted in a complete change in attitude to Western culture and technology. Prior to this the old feudal samurai regime had been totally hostile to all things Western, including railways, so it was not until 1872 that Japan opened its first railway. Built by British engineers, it ran from Tokyo to Yokohama on 1067mm GAUGE, which became the standard gauge of Japanese Imperial Railways. This narrow

gauge was later to cause Japanese National Railways (JNR) many problems.

A period of rapid expansion ensued, and by 1890, 1458 miles (2348km) of track were in operation. At this point, State and private enterprise were both involved in railway building, but in 1891, the government assumed control for the planning and construction of main lines. This involved compulsory purchase of seventeen private lines, although the private companies were granted a great deal of autonomy for the construction and building of branch lines. In 1908, the Railway Board was established, followed by a Ministry of Railways in 1920 which was absorbed into the Ministry of Transport in 1945. In 1949, the system became a public corporation—Japanese National Railways.

Although JNR has always received substantial investment from the government, by the late 1970s, it had run up an accumulated loss of around £7 billion. Although the much admired SHINKANSEN trains (running on 1435mm gauge lines and inaugurated in the 1960s) have proved extremely profitable, these profits have been swallowed up in the losses resulting from the old 1067mm gauge which comprises the bulk of the system. The narrow gauge posed huge restrictions on the development of high-speed and large-capacity vehicles which could have competed with road haulage, and resulted in the loss of much of JNR's freight business. To compound its problems, passengers had not paid an economically viable fare, even where discounts (such as those available by statute to students and commuters) were not in operation. The situation had reached crisis levels by 1976, when the government finally pressurized the legislative assembly into allowing JNR to set its own fare levels (subject to approval by the Ministry of Transport) providing they remained within the rate of inflation. Immediately, fares were increased by 50% and levels of discount reduced substantially, although this did little to clear debts already incurred.

With privatization in mind, the JNR was split into seven different operational groups in 1987 under the title of Japanese Railways Group. The West Japan Railway Co. (JR West) has 2771 miles (4463km) of 1067mm gauge and 400 miles (645km) of 1435mm gauge (Shinkansen.) The Hokkaido Railway Co. (JR Hokkaido) has 1632 miles (2628km) of 1067 gauge. The Kyushu Railway Co (JR Kyushu) has 1305 miles (2101km) of 1067mm gauge, and opened its first Shinkansen line from Yatushiro to Kayoshima in 1991. The Central Japan Railway Co. (JR Central) has 888 miles (1431km) of 1067 gauge and 343 miles (553km) of 1,435mm gauge (Tokaido Shinkansen), and the Shikoku Railway Co. (JR Shikoku) has 531 miles (856km) of 1067mm track. The East Japan Railway Co. (JR East) has 4138 miles (6663km) of 1067mm gauge and 521 miles (839km) of 1435mm gauge (Shinkansen). Japan Freight Railway Co. handles all freight traffic—about 61.6 million tons annually.

jazz trains
The name given to the GREAT WESTERN RAILWAY's cheap service introduced to compete with ELECTRIFICATION on London's Liverpool Street West Side suburban services in the 1920s.

Jeannie Deans
The Jeannie Deans was one of Francis WEBB's three cylinder COMPOUND LOCOMOTIVES which he built for the London and North Western Railway. It reliably pulled the Euston to Glasgow express every day from 1891 to 1899.

Jenny Lind
Designed by David Joy and John Fenton in 1846, the Jenny Lind was a 2–2–2 which became an extremely successful passenger locomotive. The layout of its axleboxes enhanced its stability, and its boiler pressure of 120 psi allowed it to achieve high speeds.

Jones, John Luther Casey (1864–1900)

John Luther Casey Jones is the American STEAM LOCOMOTIVE driver who has been immortalized in a folk song by Wallace Saunders, a locomotive cleaner. On 30 April 1900, Jones was driving his Cannonball Express train from Memphis to Canton in Mississippi. Driving at full speed, Jones' engine crashed into the rear of a freight train. Jones died in the collision but his crew and passengers all survived because of decisive action he had taken in slowing down the train once he realised that the crash was in evitable. Despite the conclusion of the crash investigators (who asserted that the collision occurred because Jones had disregarded signals), Jones was regarded as a hero and Saunders' song became extremely popular throughout America.

Joy, David (1825–1903)

David Joy (together with John Fenton) designed the JENNY LIND type 2–2–2. Its special arrangement of axleboxes gave it greater stability at speed, and it soon gained fame as one of the more reliable expresses of the day. He is also remembered for the Joy radial valve gear, adopted by the LONDON AND NORTH WESTERN and the Lancashire and Yorkshire Railways.

Judah, Theodore (1826–1863)

Judah was engineer to the American Central Pacific Railroad, and was instrumental in the driving of a line across the Sierra Nevada, which ultimately facilitated the building of the first transcontinental railway in the US.

K

Kaiser Ferdinand Nordbahn

The Austrian statesman Prince Metternich enlisted the help of the banking magnate Salomon de Rothschild to help persuade the Austro-Hungarian Emperor, Kaiser Ferdinand I to consider building the empire's first railway. The result was the Kaiser Ferdinand Nordbahn, which opened on 6 January 1838 and ran from Vienna to Deutsch Wagram and Florisdorf.

key
The block of pressed oak or steel which secures the rail into its cast-iron chair.

Kilmarnock and Troon Railway
The Kilmarnock and Troon was the first real railway in Scotland. It was incorporated in May 1808, and opened on 6 July 1812, operating horse traction until steam power was introduced in 1817.

king lever
A SIGNALLING lever which permits signals to be operated remotely from another box, or to operate automatically by means of the track circuits. The signals in its own box are cut out or bypassed.

Kirtley, Matthew (1813–73)
Kirtley was the first locomotive superintendent of the Midland Railway from 1844. His 2–4–0 Midland types were among the few standard-gauge locomotives which could rival the Great Western's single drivers for speed and hauling capability. He also combined the FIREBOX brick arch with the deflector plate to permit the replacement of coke with coal.

kylchap exhaust system
The exhaust system developed by Andre CHAPÉLON. With its double blastpipe and chimney it increased draught and minimized back pressure, thereby greatly improving locomotive efficiency.

L

ladder
A track layout which permits crossing over a series of parallel lines and is simpler and more cost-effective than the old system of diamond crossings and doubler slips.

land cruise
A term originally used by a New York travel agent in 1925 to describe special tours made by trains known as 'hotel trains'. These trains were equipped with similar facilities such as those which would be found on a cruise liner. The GREAT WESTERN RAILWAY also adopted the phrase 'land cruise' in 1927 to describe tours made by special trains and road coaches and including hotel accommodation. Later, BRITISH RAIL organized so-called 'land cruises' around North Wales in summer between 1950 and 1961. These were simply circular day trips, sometimes with radio commentaries.

Linz-Budweis Railway
A section of the Linz-Budweis railway opened on 7 September 1827 and ran from Budweis (then in Bohemia but now Ceske Budejovice in the Czech Republic) to Travnov using horse traction. This railway was most probably the first public railway in mainland Europe. Later (in 1854) it became the first NARROW-GAUGE public railway in Europe to use steam traction.

Lion
The Lion was a locomotive built by Todd, Kitson and Laird of Leeds, based on the design of the PATENTEE.

Liverpool (Bury)
The 0–4–0 Liverpool was built by Edward BURY in 1830. It was the first locomotive to have a bar frame (which was later

adopted as standard American practice) and a haycock FIREBOX. Liverpool was sold to the St Petersburg Railway in 1833.

Liverpool (Crampton)
The locomotive 6–2–0 Liverpool was built by Thomas CRAMPTON in 1848 for the LONDON AND NORTH WESTERN RAILWAY. The use of a long BOILER and large wheels to the rear of the FIREBOX enabled this standard gauge locomotive to become the first to rival the speed of the broad-gauge locomotives. Unfortunately, it tended to damage the rails and was withdrawn and abandoned in Britain. It was, however, adopted and adapted very successfully by the French.

Liverpool and Manchester Railway
The Liverpool and Manchester was incorporated on 5 May 1826 and opened on 15 September 1830. This opening was a landmark in that the Liverpool and Manchester was really the world's first modern main-line railway. It used mechanical traction alone to convey goods and passengers, and, unlike other companies, the railway handled all the traffic by itself as opposed to leasing out track and services. In 1829, the famous RAINHILL TRIALS were held on the railway to establish that the STEAM LOCOMOTIVE was indeed a reliable form of power for the railways.

loading gauge
Early British civil engineers on the railways had the foresight to envisage a day when trains would be capable of traversing the length and breadth of the country at speeds far in excess of any attained by those for which they were designing. Consequently, engineers tunnelled and built bridges over and through topographical obstacles to avoid lengthening, bending or grading a route. Unfortunately, they failed to envisage that one day engines might of necessity be much larger in order to obtain these

projected speeds. The effect of this unfortunate lack of foresight is that Britain now has a multitude of bridges and tunnels, and thousands of miles of track with the most restrictive of clearances. (The notable exception being the GREAT WESTERN RAILWAY which was initially built to accommodate BRUNEL's broad gauge.) This has had the effect of preventing British designers after World War I from emulating and developing some of the larger and more powerful engines produced by their continental counterparts. A comparison of some loading gauges is given below.

British Loading Gauge
12ft 11ins vehicle height (3.95m)
9ft 0ins vehicle width (2.75m)

Berne Loading Gauge (Mainland Europe)
14ft 09ins vehicle height (4.5m)
10ft 02ins vehicle width (3.2m)

North American Loading Gauge
16ft 02ins vehicle height (4.9m)
10ft 10ins vehicle width (3.3m)

Old USSR Railways
17ft 04ins vehicle height (5.3m)
11ft 02ins vehicle width (3.4m)

Locomotion

The Locomotion was a locomotive built by Robert STEPHENSON which succeeded in pulling a record load of 69 tons from Shildon to Stockton in 1825.

London and Birmingham Railway

The London and Birmingham was the first main-line railway into London to be completed. The railway opened in its entirety on 17 September 1838.

London and Greenwich Railway

The London and Greenwich Railway was London's first railway and opened on 8 February 1836. It ran from Spa Road to Deptford. It later extended to London Bridge in December of that year, and to Greenwich in 1838.

London and North Eastern Railway

The LNER was created at the time of AMALGAMATION in 1923. Amongst many smaller private railways, it incorporated Great Central Railway, Great Eastern Railway, Great North of Scotland Railway, Great Northern Railway, NORTH BRITISH RAILWAY and North Eastern Railway. It eventually became part of BRITISH RAIL in 1948.

London and North Western Railway

The London and North Western Railway was one of the larger pre-AMALGAMATION railways, formed in 1846 and recorded as having 2063 route miles (3322km) in 1914. It became part of the LONDON, MIDLAND AND SCOTTISH RAILWAY after AMALGAMATION in 1923.

London, Midland and Scottish Railway

One of the 'big four' railways created at AMALGAMATION in 1923. The London, Midland and Scottish was formed from the old LONDON AND NORTH WESTERN RAILWAY, the Midland Railway, and various smaller railways.

Ludwigsbahn

The Ludwigsbahn was the first railway in what is now Germany. It opened on 7 December 1835 and ran between Fürth and Nuremberg, using steam power to convey its passengers at the outset. Due to a failure of a German firm to deliver a locomotive on time, the Ludwigsbahn's first locomotive was Der Adler, a STEPHENSON engine built along the lines of the PATENTEE. The line proved so successful that it convinced many in

Germany who had been sceptical of the new form of transport, and some of Germany's first main lines were laid within just a few years of Der Adler's debut.

M

Maglev trains
Maglev trains operate by means of magnetic levitation. This is a real departure from traditional railway design, as the cars have no wheels and are designed to rise above the track by means of electromagnets. The great advantage of these vehicles is that there are no working parts to wear out, as the train does not come into contact with the track when it is in motion. A Maglev train service opened in Birmingham in the 1980s, operating between the airport and Birmingham International Railway Station.

main line
The term given either to any part of the track upon which trains run, excluding sidings and yards, or to any of the major lines connecting the cities and larger towns.

Mallard
GRESLEY's Class A4 Pacific which attained the world speed record of 126mph (78km/h) in 1937—a feat never surpassed by a STEAM LOCOMOTIVE.

Mallet
The name given to Anatole MALLET's STEAM LOCOMOTIVES which were fitted with a single boiler but also had two sets of coupled driving wheels. The design was particularly popular in the US, where it was developed by the Union Pacific's 540-ton 'Big

Boys'. These 4-8-8-4 locomotives were the world's largest, and were widely used to carry troops between 1941 and 1944.

Mallet, Anatole (1837–1919)

Anatole Mallet was a French locomotive engineer who invented the COMPOUND ENGINE, which was patented in 1884. His engine had a fixed rear engine unit with high-pressure cylinders and a swivel front engine unit which carried the low-pressure cylinders. Its main advantage was that it could use the steam twice, thereby saving on coal.

Manchester and Leeds Railway

The Manchester and Leeds opened on 1 March 1841, making it the first railway across the Pennines.

marshalling

The breaking up and reassembling of trains in preparation for their journeys. It is usually carried out in marshalling yards.

match truck

A wagon with BUFFERS at either end which can be coupled to vehicles at each end without the need for them to have buffers or drawgear of the same height. The term match truck is also used to describe a wagon with a load which overhangs it.

Mexican railways

The first Mexican railway opened in 1873 and ran from Veracruz to Mexico City. It had 1435mm GAUGE and involved a climb of over 2400mm with gradients of 1 in 25.

In 1908, the National Railroad of Mexico and Mexican Central Railways merged to form Mexican National Railways (Ferrocarriles Nacionales de Mexico). By 1987 FNdeM had absorbed all the railways of Mexico to form a system with a total route length of 12,610 miles (20,306km) most of which 1435mm gauge and the remaining is 914mm gauge.

Middleton Railway

The Middleton Railway, Leeds has the distinction of being the wagonway authorized by the first ever Railway Act in Britain. Steam traction was introduced in 1812, using BLENKINSOP's toothed wheel and rack propulsion system.

monorail

As their title suggests, monorail trains travel along a single rail or beam which provides a supporting structure. The car is usually designed to straddle the rail and runs on electric power. The power is collected from strips of conductive material fitted to either side of the rail or beam. These compact and flexible railways had many uses, and have proved popular for transporting people around leisure parks, airports and exhibitions.

Murray, Matthew (1765–1826)

A mechanical engineer, Murray established an engineering works which manufactured textile machinery and steam engines of his design. He built the first commercially successful steam locomotive (1811–13) for the Middleton Colliery Railway using the rack system designed by John BLENKINSOP.

N

Naples to Portici Railway

The Naples to Portici was the first railway in Italy. It opened on 4 October 1839.

narrow-gauge railways

A narrow-gauge railway is simply one with less than the 1435mm standard gauge. In the early days of the developing railway system, narrow-gauge lines were constructed where the terrain would not permit construction of standard gauge, either for physical or financial reasons. They were extremely flexible, being able to negotiate much tighter bends than normal trains and enabling the use of much lighter earthworks and bridges.

Initially, narrow-gauge lines were principally used for the conveyance of stone or slate and minerals, transporting their loads from the production site to the nearest main line or port. However, the narrow-gauge also provided essential passenger trains where the standard gauge could not cope with the terrain of some remote areas.

Not all narrow gauge locomotives had to be small—in fact the 1066mm lines of South Africa required equipment which was often just as large (and sometimes larger) than that of some standard gauge lines. One of the best-known narrow gauge locomotives was the Garratt type (built by Beyer-Peacock of Manchester) which was specially designed to provide stability, power and flexibility on a lighter weight of track. For many private British companies, supplying the narrow-gauge worldwide provided the mainstay of their trade.

The FFESTINIOG RAILWAY was the first narrow gauge railway to adopt the use of steam locomotives. It transported slate from the Blaenau Ffestiniog quarries to Porthmadog. Another first for the Ffestiniog was the use of bogie carriages from 1870—the first in Britain to do so. Today the Ffestiniog is a thriving and well-preserved private passenger line.

The narrowest gauge acceptable for practical use is generally agreed to be 381mm, that developed by the Victorian gentleman engineer Sir Arthur Heywood . He devised many of these minimum-gauge lines for military, estate and industrial work. These have been superseded by the internal combustion engine but some still remain in use for pleasure. The best known examples are probably the Ravenglass and Eskdale Railway and the Romney, Hythe and Dymchurch Railway.

nationalization

The Second World War inflicted irreparable damage on the already beleaguered rail system. In addition to the ferrying of troops to and from the south coast, considerable damage was also sustained as a result of air raids. However, with the war's end the old order had changed—a Labour government firmly committed to nationalization was returned to power. The old railways were bought by compulsory purchase under the Transport Act of 1947, and on 1 January 1948, BRITISH RAILWAYS was born.

British Railways was divided up into six administrative regions with overall control retained by the BRITISH TRANSPORT COMMISSION. The main priority in the early days was to repair the damage done by the war and to try to restore services as far as possible to pre-war standards. Considering the condition of the British economy in the immediate post-war years, this must have seemed like a fairly insurmountable task. However, the government was aware of the importance of the railways to the recovery of the nation and to society as a whole, and set about freeing the railways from some of the obstacles which had hampered it in the past. In 1953, a Transport Act was passed which permitted the railways more freedom in fixing their rates and also devolved power to the regional managers.

It became apparent too that economies had to be made. Between 1948 and 1959, almost 3000 miles (4831km) of unprofitable lines were closed, either completely or to passengers only. By closing unnecessary stations, savings were made in both money and time and electrification was expanded. However, the commission was aware of the system's shortcomings and announced the Modernization Plan in 1955, which was intended to provide for long-term development.

non stop

The term normally given to a train which travels between two points without any passenger stops. The term is often falsely used to describe a train omitting only one or two stops on its journey.

non-token lock and block
This method of working a single line was first introduced by the Sykes' Interlocking Signal Co. in 1905. Basically, the signals would not permit a train to enter a defined section without the clear signal being first sanctioned by a signalman at the other end of the section. Once the train has been permitted to enter the section, the signal would automatically register 'danger' and would remain unchanged until the train had quit the section, thereby releasing the instruments. It would, however, be up to the signalman to check that each train was complete upon leaving the section, as the system did not allow for elements of the train becoming accidentally detached.

Nord Express
This service was introduced by the COMPAGNIE INTERNATIONALE DES WAGONS LITS in 1896 and ran between Paris and St Petersburg via Ostend and Berlin. It originally used DE GLEHN compound 4–4–0s and was able to average speeds of 55mph between Paris and St Quentin including stops—a feat which was extremely impressive by the standards of the day. However, the two world wars severely disrupted the service by truncating the route, and in 1946, the Nord Express was re-routed to run from Paris to Stockholm via Ostend, Hamburg and Copenhagen. From 1986, the route ran from Ostend to Copenhagen only.

North British Railway
The North British Railway was incorporated in 1844, and the first section opened between Edinburgh, Berwick and Haddington in 1846. By 1914 it operated more than 1375 route miles, the bulk of which was in Eastern and Central Scotland. It became part of LONDON AND NORTH EASTERN RAILWAY in 1923.

North Eastern Railway

The North Eastern Railway was incorporated in 1854 and included the old York, Newcastle and Berwick Railway, the Malton and Driffield Railway, the York and North Midland Railway and the Leeds Northern Railway. At its zenith in 1914, the North Eastern Railway operated approximately 1249 route miles (2011km), mostly in Durham, Yorkshire and Northumberland. Upon amalgamation, in 1923, the North Eastern Railway became part of LONDON AND NORTH EASTERN RAILWAY.

North London Railway

The North London Railway was incorporated in 1846 as the East and West India Docks and Birmingham Junction Railway and opened its first sections in 1850 and 1851. The name changed to North London Railway in 1853, and the railway was to all intents and purposes controlled by the LONDON AND NORTH WESTERN RAILWAY until it was completely absorbed by the railway in 1922.

North Union Railway

The North Union Railway, Lancashire, was the result the amalgamation of the Wigan Branch line and the Wigan and Preston railways in 1834. The Act of Amalgamation was the first such Act in this country.

North Star

The North Star was built for the broad-gauge GREAT WESTERN RAILWAY by Robert STEPHENSON in 1837. Based on the PATENTEE design, it proved a great success and continued in service until 1870.

Northumbrian

The Northumbrian was built by the STEPHENSONS in the 1830s and was the first locomotive to have its FIREBOX integral to the BOILER.

O

observation car
A special coach with huge windows, and often including end windows and an open balcony, so designed to afford passengers an unobstructed view of scenery.

occupation crossing/level crossing
A crossing provided by a landowner to allow crossing of a railway which divides the land.

ocean terminal
A terminal opened in 1950 to provide facilities for passengers on boat trains connecting with ocean liners. The building contained a VIP lounge, customs halls and two reception halls. The original building was demolished in 1963, but some ocean terminal facilities are still in existence.

on company's service
A marking on a package or FREIGHT item which indicates that it is permitted to travel free.

Office Centrale des Transports Internationaux par Chemins de Fer/OCTI
The international office governing the application of international conventions on freight, passenger and parcel carriage by rail. It also has a conciliatory role in relation to disputes concerning conventions.

Osterreichische Bundesbahnen
Austrian Federal Railways.

Oystermouth Railway
The Oystermouth Railway or Tramroad Company was incorpo-

rated on 29 June 1804. It opened in 1806, and ran from Swansea to Mumbles in South Wales. The following year, it became the first railway anywhere in the world to cater for fare-paying passengers. It used horse power right up until 1877 when it introduced steam traction. From 1929 onwards, the Oystermouth Railway ran as an electric tramway, until it closed on 5 January 1960.

P

Pakistani railways
Pakistan's first railway opened in 1861 and ran from Karachi to Kotri, although at that time it formed part of India's North Western Railway. When India was partitioned, the North Western became the Pakistan Western Railway. A further change was necessitated in 1974, when the eastern part of Pakistan became Bangladesh. The title was then changed to Pakistan Railways. Pakistan railways has approximately 5448 miles (8,774km) of 1676mm gauge line and 276 miles (445km) of 762mm gauge.

Parcels and Miscellaneous Van/PMV
A British Rail van designed to carry parcels etc., with end and side doors and no gangway.

passenger services
In Britain, the first railways recorded as having carried passengers in addition to goods was the OYSTERMOUTH RAILWAY and the KILMARNOCK AND TROON. These were horsedrawn passenger services; the first railway to carry passengers by steam locomotive was the STOCKTON AND DARLINGTON in 1825. Passengers were not carried on a regular basis although the Stockton and Darlington had obtained an Act of Parliament to permit it to do

so, and it still used horse power occasionally. In fact, passenger revenue amounted to only a third of the total, as coal was still seen as the mainstay of the railway.

However, the Stockton and Darlington did arouse great interest in the possibilities of passenger transport, and the LIVERPOOL AND MANCHESTER was the first to operate passenger services using entirely mechanical traction. With original projections of 700 passengers per day, the Liverpool and Manchester actually averaged around 1,100 passengers daily between 1831–33.

Early railway coaches were built to resemble the existing mode of passenger transport—the stagecoach—as closely as possible. Their bodywork and appearance was virtually identical to that of the horsedrawn carriage. Coaches such as these, however, were intended only for wealthy passengers paying premium fares. The rest had to travel along with the luggage on the roof of these coaches, or on open wagons. These early wagons were often completely devoid of seats and protection from the elements—save some rudimentary holes drilled in the floor to permit the drainage of rain water. The development of verandah-type roofs on some of these wagons heralded the advent of second-class rail travel.

Second-class travel in compartment coaches did not appear until 1837. These were far from luxurious, however, having no refreshment or toilet facilities. Fortunately, schedules stops tended to be frequent at this time, and some stations gradually began to take pride in the provision of dining and other passenger facilities.

The first passenger carriages to run on low pivoted trucks or bogies were designed by Ross Winans, a New Jersey farmer. This permitted the use of a much larger car, and the first of these went into service for the BALTIMORE AND OHIO RAILROAD in 1831. The length of this vehicle permitted saloon-style seating with a central gangway, a development seized upon by Tsar Nicholas I

passenger services

who invited Winans to set up a car-construction works at Alesandrovsk.

No such improvements had reached Britain and the rest of Europe by the end of the Great Exhibition in 1851. Rail travel had rendered the stagecoach all but obsolete in Britain, and some 80,000,000 travellers used the railways each year. Cheap fares meant that working class people could make previously unattainable journeys and holidays away gradually became a feature of life for many. Despite this, a second class passenger on a GREAT WESTERN RAILWAY train died of cold and exposure, whilst third-class passengers were still herded onto goods wagons where they huddled together perilously on planks.

In 1844, William GLADSTONE attempted to provide for third class passengers in a Parliamentary Act which insisted that all new railways provide at least one third class train daily—some had refused to provide any service at all for third class passengers—and that carriages were to have proper seats with protection from the weather. Companies were generally reluctant to improve the lot of the third class traveller, often laying on only one train at a ridiculously early hour, until 1872, when the Midland announced that it was to take third class passengers on all of its trains. Its rivals greeted this announcement with howls of derision, but were gradually compelled by the success of the venture to fall into line. In 1874, the Midland again confounded its competitors by completely abolishing third class and lowering the first class fare to second class rates. A year later it upholstered all its third class carriages. These moves were not so much based on altruism as a clear vision and appreciation of the potentially vast profits to be made. Political emancipation, improved standards of living and the spread of the railways themselves was opening up a huge market in rail travel for ordinary working people—a market which the Midland was quick to exploit.

Other railways gradually followed suit, albeit somewhat reluctantly at times, and it was indeed the desire to cater for the masses rather than the privileged few which led to the improvements which came to be taken for granted by the 20th century passenger—such as lavatories, restaurant cars and corridor coaches.

Patentee
The Patentee was a STEAM LOCOMOTIVE built by the STEPHENSON & Co., in 1834, and its design was to have a lasting influence on other designers. It featured two CYLINDERs driving a central axle and strong frames outside the wheels.

payload
That part of a train's total hauled weight which earns revenue.

Peacock, Richard (1820–89)
Peacock became locomotive superintendent on the Leeds and Selby Railway at just 18 years of age before moving on to the Sheffield, Ashton and Manchester Railway. He set up the locomotive works at Gorton in Manchester prior to forming a partnership with Charles BEYER. Gorton became the location for their famous locomotive building firm, Beyer-Peacock, which supplied STEAM LOCOMOTIVES to railways throughout the world.

peak hours
The busiest periods of the day in traffic terms, i.e., day and night.

Pease, Edward (1767–1858)
Pease was an astute businessman and Quaker financier who supported George STEPHENSON from his early days as an engineer, and promoted the STOCKTON AND DARLINGTON RAILWAY. He was also a co-founder of the locomotive building firm of Stephenson & Co., in 1823.

pedestal frame
In a signal box, the pedestal frame is a framework supporting the shelf of block instruments.

Pendelzug
The German name for a PUSH AND PULL TRAIN.

Pendolino
An Italian train, designed by Fiat, that uses the PENDULAR SUSPENSION system.

pendular suspension
A suspension system in which the coach bodies tilt slightly to aid negotiation of curves.

peripheral station
An outer suburban stop on a main line enabling passengers to avoid travelling all the way to a city centre.

permanent way
The name given to all track, including SLEEPERS, rails, fastenings and BALLAST in order to distinguish it from temporary tracks laid during construction.

permissive block
A variation of BLOCK SYSTEM working in which more than one train is permitted to enter a block section. The system is only ever used for freight trains, and normally at very low speeds.

Pest-Vacz Railway
The Pest-Vacz Railway was the first railway in Hungary. It opened on 15 July 1844.

Phoenix
The Phoenix, built by the Stephenson & Co., in 1830, was the first engine to have a SMOKEBOX. It was used by the LIVERPOOL AND MANCHESTER RAILWAY.

piggy-back
A freight system in which special low-loader flat wagons carry complete fully loaded road vehicles or road trailers.

Planet
The Planet was a locomotive built by the Stephenson & Co., in 1830 for the LIVERPOOL AND MANCHESTER RAILWAY. Among its more notable features were outside bearings and sandwich frames, and CYLINDERS enclosed within the FIREBOX.

pneumatic railway
Another name for the ATMOSPHERIC RAILWAY.

points
The parts of the rails which move thereby deciding the route followed by the train. A train will be turned to the right (from a position facing the points) by a right hand set of points, and a left hand set will turn a train to the left.

Polish Railways
The Warsaw-Vienna railway was the first to be built in what is now Poland, although at the time (1842) it was divided between Austro-Hungary, Prussia and Russia. Poland regained its independence in 1918, and since then its railways have been known as Polish State Railways (Polskie Koleje Panstwowe/PKP). In 1918, PKP had 10,158 miles (16,359km) of track comprising both 1435mm and 1524mm gauges. At the end of the Second World War in 1945, alteration to national boundaries expanded PKP's total route length. In 1991, the total was 16,546 miles (26,644km) of which 15,082 miles (24,287km) was 1435mm gauge, 1463 miles (2357km) NARROW GAUGE and 306 miles (493km) of 1524mm gauge.

pop safety valve
A valve which makes a characteristic 'pop' sound as it releases

a large amount of steam in order to maintain a pre-set boiler pressure.

Portable Ticket Issuing Service/PORTIS
The issuing system used where conductors operate on rural or suburban services.

porter
A railway employee who was employed on manual duties at stations, such as assisting passengers with luggage, closing and opening train doors and general tidying. BRITISH RAIL dispensed with the term in favour of railman/woman.

postal services
Although the stagecoaches of the Royal Mail had provided a remarkably speedy and efficient service in its time, it soon became evident that the new form of transport could offer great advances in speed and efficiency. The first mail was carried by rail on 11 November 1830 by the LIVERPOOL AND MANCHESTER RAILWAY. Eventually, the government empowered the General Post Office to send mail by any train, although a special mail train was the preferred option.

The possibility of actually sorting mail in transit had been vaunted during stagecoach days, but the limitations of space prevented this from ever becoming a serious option. It was quite obviously a practical proposition on the railway, and the first Travelling Post Office (TPO) was run on the Grand Junction Railway in 1838. Postal workers in the TPO coaches carried out most of the function normally carried out in a post office—much as they do today. Clearly much time is saved by sorting the mail as it travels towards its destination, and further time was saved by the use of special apparatus attached to the train and situated on the lineside. This apparatus took the form of nets designed to enable the train to deposit mailbags on the move. A special pouch suspended from a lineside arm permitted collection of mail onto the train, again without stopping. This system was last used in 1971, as road vehicles usurped their function. Today, there are more than thirty TPOs covering approximately 5,500,000 miles (8,856,680km) every year.

power box
An electrically powered signal box, in which thumb switches and miniature levers are used in conjunction with electrical interlocking.

Prairie
An American 2–6–2 STEAM LOCOMOTIVE.

preserved railway/private tourist railway
A term given to an abandoned railway or line which has been restored to operational service by enthusiasts, usually using restored steam or diesel rolling stock. Occasionally, a railway will be specially constructed for leisure and tourism purposes. These are usually geared to seasonal working for the benefit of tourists and depend heavily on volunteers to man them. *See* PRESERVED, PRIVATE AND TOURIST RAILWAYS on page 179.

privatization
The British Government formally announced its intention to privatize the railways in 1992 and set about breaking up the system by way of preparation. The resulting sectors were InterCity, Network South East and a variety of regional networks. The Railways Bill of 1993 received Royal Assent in 1993 despite universal opposition from public and politicians alike.

Since April 1994, RAILTRACK has owned the track, stations and signalling and is responsible for their smooth operation and maintenance. It is envisaged that around 25 sections of the existing network will be offered for sale to private franchisees who will pay a toll to Railtrack in order to run their trains.

Puffing Billy

The first commercially successful STEAM LOCOMOTIVE, Puffing Billy was designed for Captain Blackett, the owner of Wylam Moor Coal and Wylam Railway, by William HEDLEY, the colliery manager. Neither mechanic nor engineer, Hedley was doubtless given much practical assistance by Timothy HACKWORTH and Jonathan Forster, the colliery smith and engineman. Puffing Billy was remarkable at the time in that it was the first engine to prove that a smooth wheel running on a smooth rail could provide adequate traction for commercial haulage. The engine can be seen at the Science Museum, London.

Pullman cars

In the early days of passenger rail travel, trains quickly became faster and bigger, but passenger coaches were often quite uncomfortable. Gradually, railway companies began to offer such comforts as light, lavatories, heating and catering in the realization that the higher the level of luxury offered, the greater the number of passengers they acquired. In the US, a businessman named George Pullman (1831–97) designed a large luxury sleeping coach called the Pioneer. Later, he introduced a luxurious dining car. These coaches were soon introduced to Europe, and Pullman soon became the byword for comfort and luxury in rail travel. Famed for their intricate woodwork and tasteful decoration, Pullman coaches had armchairs, glass-topped tables and brass lamps. The attendant could be summoned by pulling a bell, and would serve meals and refreshments at each seat.

Pullman Open/PO

The name given to the First Class British Rail INTERCITY 125 Mark 3 coach.

push and pull train

One which may be driven from either end.

Q

Q-Train
A train introduced in 1983 which is manned by officers of the British Transport Police where there is a likelihood of violence or vandalism.

Quintinshill
The worst disaster in British rail history occured at Quintinshill, north of Carlisle, in 1915. More than 220 people died as the result of a collision between two trains.

R

rack railway
A mechanical system whereby steel teeth fitted continuously in the track mesh with cogs or pinion wheels on the locomotive. The increased traction helps trains negotiate extremely steep gradients.

rail grinder
A vehicle designed to smooth out irregularities on the rails, usually fitted with carborundum blocks.

rails
Since early times, man used some sort of plank to move a vehicle with wheels to transport a load over rough or soft ground. This is still the basic principle on which the modern railway is founded. For many hundreds of years, the simple method of plank and wheel was used, until the late-18th century. In the 1780s and 90s, the first wheels with guiding FLANGES appeared

and were used in conjunction with wooden rails protected with metal straps. In the absence of flanged wheels, a cast iron plate was developed to keep the wheels on track. Gradually, the term railway (which had originally been used to refer to timber tracks) came to cover all plateways, wagonways and tramways.

Railtrack

Railtrack was created in 1994 as part of the British government's plan for privatization of the railways. A government-owned company, Railtrack owns all track, signalling and stations and will exact a toll for their use from private franchisees.

In the first three years since its inception, Railtrack has been severely criticized by the rail regulator for underspending by several millions—a charge which is disputed by Railtrack's chairman. In February 1997, Railtrack announced that it was to spend £15.9 billion over the next ten years on improvements, including track and bridge span renewal. It also proposes a large capacity FREIGHT route for the CHANNEL TUNNEL to Scotland.

Railway King, The
See HUDSON, GEORGE.

Rainhill Trials

The famous Rainhill Trials were held at Rainhill on the Liverpool and Manchester Railway in October 1929. The directors of the railway (as with other railway directors countrywide) had little confidence in the reliability of the new steam locomotives and were tempted to use stationary steam engines hauling rope instead. Horrified at this prospect the George and Robert STEPHENSON persuaded the directors to hold a contest which was meant to demonstrate once and for all the reliability of steam. Locomotive designers and builders were invited to submit entries for competitive trial with a prize of £500 for the winner. Three entrants turned up on the day—Sans Pareil, designed by

Timothy HACKWORTH, Novelty designed by John Braithwaite and John Ericsson and ROCKET designed by the Stephensons. Although Novelty managed an impressive 40mph (64.4km/h) to Rocket's 29.5mph (47.5km/h), Rocket was the overall winner in terms of reliability and overall performance.

Red Star
A profitable division of BRITISH RAIL's parcels group which aimed to deliver registered parcels on the same day they were received by using the fastest available trains.

Rede Nacionale de los Ferrocarriles Espanoles/RENFE
Spanish National Railways.

regulator (handle)
The valve which gives the driver of a STEAM LOCOMOTIVE control over the amount of steam admitted from the BOILER to the steam chest. The 'fully position' permits the maximum amount of steam to enter.

release key
A key which enables a signalman to override the mechanical and electrical safety devices on a lock-and-block system.

Riddles, Robert Arthur (1892–1983)
In 1909, Robert Arthur Riddles began his training as a locomotive engineer with LONDON AND NORTH WESTERN RAILWAY. He gained prominence with the LONDON, MIDLAND AND SCOTTISH RAILWAY, and whilst in charge of the Ministry of Supply's Directorate of Transport, he designed 935 2–8–0s and 150 2–10–0s which were built for the War Department. When BRITISH RAIL was formed on 1 January 1948, he became its chief mechanical and electrical engineer and was responsible for the design of all British Rail's standard STEAM LOCOMOTIVES. He (unsuccessfully) supported the idea of ELECTRIFICATION for the railways rather

than replacing steam completely by DIESEL TRACTION. He retired from British Rail in 1953.

Rocket
Rocket was the engine which won the RAINHILL TRIALS in 1829. Designed largely by George STEPHENSON, Rocket was not the fastest entrant in the competition but by far the most reliable.

Romanian railways
Romania's first railway was opened in 1869 and ran from Bucharest to Giurgiu on 1435mm GAUGE track. In 1888 the railways were transferred to the state and became Romanian State Railways (Societatea Nationala a Cailor Ferate Romane–SNCFR) with 1535 miles (2472km) total route distance. Following the redistribution of territory after the First World War, the total route length was increased to 6912 miles (11,130km). The railways were designated an autonomous state enterprise in 1991, having previously been a department in the Ministry of Transport. Today the route length is approximately 7048 miles (11,350km), 6753 miles (10,876km) of which is 1435mm gauge, 28 miles (45km) 1524mm gauge and 294 miles (474km) 762mm and 610mm gauge.

Romney, Hythe and Dymchurch Railway
One of Britain's best-known preserved railways, in Kent. *See* PRESERVED, PRIVATE AND TOURIST RAILWAYS on page 179.

Royal Scot
The name given to an express train which runs between London and Glasgow/Edinburgh. After ELECTRIFICATION in 1989, the route time was shortened to 4 hrs and 52 mins.

Royal trains
Trains financed by the exchequer and made up of special rolling stock provided for the royal family.

Russian railways

The first Russian railway opened in 1837 and ran from St Petersburg to Tsarskoe Selo, the residence of the then Tsar, Nicholas I. Its engineer, the Austrian von Gerstner, predicted that its annual number of passengers would be in the region of 800,000—a figure which it very nearly achieved in its first year of operation. Spurred on by its success, the Tsar approved the construction of a 1435mm GAUGE line from Warsaw to Vienna, which was eventually completed in 1848 despite a crippling lack of finance. Notwithstanding the dire state of communications in their vast and unnavigable country, many reactionaries in the Tsar's government were totally averse to any diversion of funds for the provision of a railway system.

The Tsar, however, was convinced of its worth and in 1841 commissioned a study of contemporary American practice and a feasibility report for the proposed St Petersburg to Moscow railway. His engineers returned with very enthusiatic reports from America and the project was eventually underway. Many thousands of serfs were coerced into completing the line by 1851, and several thousands of them were said to have died in the process—often killed off by frequent outbreaks of the typhoid virus.

Upon the advice of the American engineer George Washington WHISTLER, the railway was built to the 1524mm gauge in line with American practice of the Southern states. Later, the gauge was standardized to 1435mm in the USA, while the 1524mm became standard in Russia and that which was to become the USSR.

By 1914, the Russian system was undoubtedly the largest in Europe, but the network was patchy and poorly coordinated. This was a direct result of its being owned and run by the State and 38 separate private companies, with no real attempt at co-operation between them.

S

St Etienne to Andrezieux Railway
The St Etienne to Andrezieux railway was the first railway to run in France. Its concession was granted in 1823, and the railway officially opened in 1828 using horse power. It began to carry passengers in 1832, and continued to use horse power until steam was introduced in 1844.

St Petersburg and Pavlovsk Railway
The Pavlovsk to Tsarskoe Selo section of the St Petersburg and Pavlovsk Railway was the first railway to open in Russia in October 1836). It ran from St Petersburg to the Tsar's residence at Tsarskoe-Selo. Using a locomotive built by Robert STEPHENSON, it enjoyed huge success in its first year with the result that the Tsar became firmly committed to a huge railway-building programme. *See also* RUSSIAN RAILWAYS.

saloon
The name given to a coach with an open seating area. The name can also be applied to coaches adapted for a specific purpose i.e. royal saloon.

Saxby, John (1821–1913)
Although Austin Chambers was probably the first to use an interlocking system for point and signal-operating mechanisms, John Saxby's version was the first to be patented in 1856. He went on to found the firm of Saxby & Farmer in partnership with J. S. Farmer which produced SIGNALLING apparatus.

Schmidt, Wilhelm (1858–1924)
Wilhelm Schmidt, a German engineer, invented the high-degree fire-tube SUPERHEATER. It greatly increased the temperature of the steam and therefore the efficiency of the engine. It was used

on most large engines throughout the world until the advent of diesel and electric engines in the 1960s.

Schweizerische Bundesbahnen/SBB
Swiss Federal Railways.

scissors crossover
A crossing between two parallel sets of tracks which resembles a pair of scissors.

Second man
An assistant driver who would travel in the cab with the regular driver on the fastest trains in case of emergency.

Séguin, Marc (1786–1875)
Marc Séguin was a French engineer who pioneered the multi-tubular BOILER and patented it in 1827. As chief engineer on the St Etienne to Lyon Railway, he built a locomotive with a multi-tubular boiler, which was indeed the first to run on the railway which opened in 1829.

semaphore
The old, obsolete system of SIGNALLING, whereby an arm or board would be raised and lowered by means of a manually operated lever in the signal box attached to a wire.

servicing
In the days of steam, an engine would be recalled to its shed approximately every ten days for routine maintenance. The locomotive would be allowed to cool down, then any scale or sediment from the water would be removed as its boiler was washed out. The BOILER tubes would also be cleaned. The FIREBOX would be thoroughly cleaned to remove as much ash and grime as possible, and once all the parts were satisfactorily cleaned, they would be inspected for wear and tear and any worn parts replaced. Occasionally, a major overhaul would be required, and

this would be carried out at a large central works such as Doncaster or Darlington.

The motive power depot would have had a large staff overseen by a Shedmaster. Skilled artisans of many disciplines would have attended the steam engine, but with the advent of diesel and electric traction, fewer sheds and workers have been required. However, locomotives are still recalled for frequent servicing by skilled workers.

Shinkansen
Japanese high-speed passenger railways built to standard gauge and using the famous BULLET trains. The first of these lines opened in 1964 from Tokyo to Osaka. The Shinkansen line now operates over 230 trains per day.

shunting
The name given to the moving around of rolling stock in order to arrange it to form a train, or to allow it to pick up or set down a load at a particular point.

siding
A section of track upon which trains do not run in operational service, but may be shunted or marshalled etc.

Siemens, Dr Ernst Werner von (1816–92)
The first ever practical electric locomotive was built by Siemens, a German electrical engineer, and displayed at the Berlin exhibition in 1879. His tiny three horse power engine collected power from a central live rail, enabling it to ferry 30 passengers at 4mph (6kph).

signalling
In the early days of the railways, the only form of signals available were hand and flag signals. These were usually carried out by special railway policemen, and in fact signalmen are still

known as bobbies in railway parlance. The South Eastern Railway and the LIVERPOOL AND MANCHESTER RAILWAY were amongst the first to introduce fixed signals. Traffic was run at fixed time intervals, and the signalman would leave the signal at danger for five minutes once the train had passed. This method worked well enough in areas where traffic was light, junctions were absent and drivers and signalmen followed their instructions faithfully, but as the network of railways expanded it became clear that more sophisticated arrangements were required. The busy London and Croydon Railway operated a disc system in which a red disc signalled stop when it was positioned at right angles to the line. The GREAT WESTERN RAILWAY adopted a version of this signal in 1841, which remained as standard until it was gradually superseded by SEMAPHORES from 1869 onwards.

Charles Hutton Gregory, engineer of the London and Croydon Railway, introduced the SEMAPHORE in 1841. The semaphore moved through a half circle, and provided clear and simple signals. To stop the train, it was positioned at right angles to its post; at 45 degrees it signalled proceed with caution and when fully lowered so it disappeared into its slot in the post, it gave the all clear.

The advent of the telegraph allowed signalmen to communicate with each other on different sections of the line. This allowed the changeover from the time system of controlling trains to that of space or blocks. By communicating through the telegraph, one signalman could tell another when a train had moved out of one block (or section of line) and into another. The basis of the system was that there should never be more than one train on a block at any time. Although the BLOCK SYSTEM was widely accepted as being the best available at the time, it was not without its critics who felt that it did not allow a signalman to use his discretion and allow him to direct two trains onto separate lines within the same block if it meant averting a

signalling

collision. This coupled with the fact that the changeover to this system from the old semaphore method was more costly than many companies would have liked, and as a result it was never adopted as universal practice.

Apart from ordering a driver to stop and go, signals also perform the function of indicating which way the points are set at a junction thus informing the driver which way the train is to go. The mechanism which ensures that the signals and points correspond is known as interlocking. Interlocking was first developed by Gregory of the London and Croydon and improved by John Saxby and Austin Chambers.

Eventually, an Act of Parliament in 1889 made interlocking and block working law, and these have remained the basic principles of modern signalling. However, the application of electricity meant that it was no longer necessary to have a signalman and a signal box on every block, and track circuiting was introduced. Track circuiting provided continuous monitoring of a train's movement via an electrified running line with distinct sections insulated from each other. A weak current passing through the rails energized an electromagnet, and this system was used to monitor the train's passage on illuminated diagrams on the signalbox. Britain was also one of the first countries to introduce coloured light signals to replace semaphore the London and North Eastern introduced electric relay interlocking in the 1930s. These compact signals show:

1. Red indicates that the driver must stop
2. Single yellow light indicates that the driver may proceed with caution but should be prepared to stop
3. Double yellow means the driver should proceed but be ready to stop at the next but one signal
4. Green means all clear.

In 1937, Liverpool Brunswick station had the first NX system.

This allowed the signalman to set up a train's route by throwing switches on his panel representing the start and end of the train's route. The system would then automatically set and interlock all the signals and points on the route by electric transmission.

Today trains are controlled by computers in an Integrated Control Centre (IECC). Computers select and set the train routes, control interlocking and can recognize trains by their individual numbers. Highly trained signalmen override the computer if the timetable is out of sequence for any reason, but are no longer required to push buttons and operate levers.

Silver Jubilee
The Silver Jubilee was Britain's first streamlined train which was pulled by 4–6–2 locomotives and ran between 1935 and 1939. The LONDON AND NORTH EASTERN RAILWAY used the title to commemorate King George V's 25 years on the throne.

Silver Link
The Silver Link was an A4 Pacific (No. 2509), designed by GRESLEY, which became the LONDON AND NORTH EASTERN RAILWAY's first high-speed train. It recorded speeds of 112.5mph (181km/h) 1935.

simple engine
Unlike a COMPOUND ENGINE, the steam passes only once through the CYLINDERS of a simple engine.

sleeper
The support which lies across the underside of the rails between them and the BALLAST. Originally made of wood, a concrete version is now the most-used in this country.

smoke deflectors
Metal plates so placed to direct the exhaust smoke away from the cab in order not to obscure the driver's vision.

smokebox
The section to the front of a locomotive housing the main steam pipes feeding the CYLINDERS, the chimney and the blastpipe.

Société Nationale de Chemin de Fer Français/SNCF
French National Railways.

South African railways
South Africa's first railway ran from Durban to Natal on 1435mm GAUGE and opened in 1860. The Natal government later took it over in 1877. In 1859, a 57 miles (92 km) line from Cape Town to Wellington was under construction, also on 1435mm gauge, but soon controversy rose over what was to be the standard gauge for the country. Some engineers favoured a narrow gauge of 762mm because of the difficult terrain which would have to be crossed. Eventually a compromise of 1067mm was reached, a gauge which was to become standard for South Africa and indeed the largest part of Central Africa. (Later this gauge was also adopted by Western Australia, Queensland, New Zealand, Indonesia and Japan as well as various small systems elsewhere.) Eventually, 2mm was lopped of this gauge in South Africa to comply with the latest rolling stock travelling at high speed.

In 1910, the four provinces of southern Africa were amalgamated into the Union of South Africa and its government merged its lines into one centrally controlled state operation. This also controlled harbours, road transport, pipelines and eventually the SA Airways. Since 1990, Transnet was created from the old SA Transport, and its rail division is now known as Spoornet. Commuter rail services are now operated by the Rail Commuter Corporation, a smaller separate company. Altogether, South African railways have 13,229 miles (21,303 km) of track.

Southern Railway

One of the 'big four' railways created at AMALGAMATION in 1923, the Southern Railway was formed from the South Eastern and Chatham Railway, the London Brighton and South Coast Railway and the London and South West Railway.

Spanish railways

Spain's first railway opened from Barcelona to Mataro in 1848 on 1676mm GAUGE track. The broad gauge was chosen because of the mountainous terrain which would have to be navigated—wider tracks would allow for bigger more powerful locomotive boilers which could cope with the gradients. By the time of the Civil War in 1936, the railways had been grouped to form four separate companies: the Madrid, Zaragoza and Alicante Railway, the Northern Railway, National Western Railway and Andalusian Railways. In 1941, all railways were nationalized with the exception of some narrow gauge lines. Spanish railways are called Rede Nacional de los Ferrocarriles Espanoles (RENFE).

RENFE has gradually narrowed most of its lines to 1668mm to give a smoother ride at high speed, and is presently considering converting all its lines to 1435mm to facilitate linking with other European systems. RENFE operates a total of 7800 miles (12,560km) of track, whilst Spanish Narrow-Gauge railways (FEVA—Ferrocarriles Espanoles de Via Estrecha) operates some 758 miles (1220km) of the 1000mm narrow-gauge system. Basque Railways (ET/FV) has operated 125 miles (202 km) of 1000mm track since 1979. Catalonia Railways (FGC) was established in 1979 to rationalize and improve the lines around Barcelona. It operates 27 miles (44 km) of 1435mm track and 87 miles (140km) of 1000mm gauge track. this includes 8 miles (13km) of 1000mm track railway, the Ribes de Freser—Nuria Railway. Four other small systems operate the remaining 17 miles (28km) of narrow-gauge lines.

Sprague, Frank Julian (1857–1934)

Sprague was originally a midshipman in the US navy who turned his energies to electrical engineering, inventing electric motors which could be fitted to BOGIES which were successfully applied to New York Elevated Railway Cars in 1884. He devised a system of controlling electric trains without locomotives.

Stanier, Sir William Arthur (1876–1965)

Sir William Stanier spent the early part of his career as a locomotive engineer at GREAT WESTERN RAILWAY's works in Swindon. In 1932, he became chief mechanical engineer to the LONDON, MIDLAND AND SCOTTISH RAILWAY. Stanier and GRESLEY dominated locomotive design in this country during a period which was truly the zenith of steam. Stanier's best known engines were the PACIFIC Princess Royal class, (an enlarged version of the King class he produced for GWR) the CORONATION (No. 6220) and the No. 6234 DUCHESS OF ABERCORN.

stations

The earliest railways had no real need for stations as we know them now—their needs were met quite adequately by inns and hotels along the routes, which were sometimes owned by the railways. Bardon Hill Station, for instance, was originally the Ashby Road Hotel situated on the Leicester and Swannington line. Initially, the railway rented a few rooms in the hotel for its passengers, before buying the entire building for conversion to a station. The LIVERPOOL AND MANCHESTER RAILWAY was the first to erect purpose built stations, one of which (Liverpool Road, Manchester) still survives as a museum of industry and science. This station shares the distinction of being the oldest surviving railway station along with the Mount Clare Station in Baltimore.

At first, most railway companies built their stations to a single-platform layout. The last station of this type to be built in this country was that in Newcastle in 1855, although it was almost obsolete by the time of its completion. Passengers were initially free to roam throughout the station and across the tracks until the British use of the footbridge became standard. Euston Station (1838) in London was the first built with separate platforms for each travel direction. By the 1840s, stations were adopting the U or head format whereby the platforms flanking the lines were joined at the end by a block which contained the complex of booking offices and waiting rooms. This formation was gradually adopted by most of the larger stations around the world. The Gare du Nord and the Gare de l'est in Paris are particularly fine examples which survive from the mid-19th century.

As railways gathered business and rail traffic increased, so a plethora of hotels, restaurants and bars were provided as an adjunct to mere booking facilities and assembly areas. As railway companies had no tradition of station building to draw upon, the design of station frontages and concourses was left to leading architects of the day, whilst the train sheds were designed by the railway engineers. As a result, there was little homogeneity in station design, with the exception that architects were generally called upon to create monumental entrances, presumably to reflect the prestige of individual railway companies. This occasionally meant that grand entrance porticoes were often commissioned at great expense, at the cost of providing decent facilities behind them. This was a criticism levelled at Philip Hardwick's design for Euston Station in London. It was eventually demolished in 1960–2 and replaced with something rather less grand, but providing for passenger comfort and ease of operations in a way which Hardwick had somewhat overlooked.

Smaller stations are characterized by the same eclecticism of design as their larger counterparts. Railway companies may have imposed some uniformity of design on their own lines, but this meant that there were at least as many styles as there were companies—and more. The GREAT WESTERN RAILWAY, for instance, preferred the classical style for those stations built between London and Reading, whilst those west of Reading were loosely based on the Tudor style with high chimneys and gables. Some railway architects were at great pains to ensure that no two buildings were alike. Frederick Barnes, an architect who worked for the North Midland Railway among others, was renowned in railway architecture for the individuality of his designs and the entirely distinct character of each of his many stations. The most important survivor of these is at Holywell junction. However, economic considerations and increasing amalgamation of small companies into larger ones meant that few railway companies gave carte blanche to architects in this way after the 1840s, and stations became ever more standardized.

This standardization still allowed for great variation between the companies, but between the wars, the increasing use of reinforced concrete meant that individuality in design declined.

steam locomotion

Until the end of the 18th century, man had relied mainly on horse, ox and mule (and indeed himself) to pull loaded wagons. Increasing industrialization and the consequent increase in output of raw materials provided an incentive to find a cheaper and faster way of moving goods, particularly coal and iron ore. The Napoleonic wars in which Britain was heavily involved at the turn of the new century placed heavy demands on horses and their fodder which meant that they became increasingly scarce and expensive commodities. Clearly, some new way of transporting coal from pithead to navigable river had to be found as those horsedrawn vehicles which were available were unable to cope with increasing demand.

The time was ripe for the development of the steam-powered locomotive, particularly as its fuel—coal—was in plentiful supply. Furthermore, the early technology already existed. In 1698, a Captain Savery had developed a primitive steam engine intended to pump water from mines, although the cylinder had to be water-cooled after each stroke. It was James WATT, however, who went on to refine and develop the steam engine. In 1769, he patented his single acting steam engine which used a condenser. He further refined this early prototype to produce the double-acting engine which had a crank and crosshead mechanism and a governor. So it was that for the first time in history that man had a reliable source of power which was independent of muscles or wind, and from this foundation Richard TREVITHICK was able to use a steam engine to drive a carriage in 1808.

steam locomotion—how it works

Although the steam locomotive was subject to many elaborate design variations from its earliest inception, the basic principles of steam locomotion are really quite simple. To obtain the steam, water in the BOILER is heated by a coal fire contained within a FIREBOX. The steam which results from the boiling of the water is diverted to a CYLINDER which contains a piston connected to a wheel by means of a connecting rod and crank. The pressure of the steam in the cylinder forces the piston to move thereby moving the wheel.

steam locomotives

Since Richard TREVITHICK's first steam locomotive took to the road in 1804, literally thousands have been designed and built throghout the world. The following chronological list concentrates mainly on British locomotives but touches on foreign engines, particularly where they exerted an influence on British design. It is by no means an exhaustive list, but attempts to include most of the locomotives which represented a milestone in the age of steam. (Some engines also have separate entries.)

steam locomotives

- **1804** Trevithick's engine pulls 15 tons
- **1805** Trevithick builds an engine with flanged wheels
- **1811** BLENKINSOP's engine successfully uses cog wheel and toothed rack rail.
- **1813** William HEDLEY's PUFFING BILLY and WYLAM DILLY are built. Hedley uses gears to power more than one set of wheels. Eventually these engines had to be rebuilt as eight-wheelers to minimize damage to the track. Wylam Dilly ran until 1866.
- **1814** George STEPHENSON's BLUCHER ran at Killingworth. Stephenson's subsequent engines use exhaust steam to intensify the heat of the firegrate and mounted the cylinders on top of the boiler thus simplifying the drive to the wheels. He dispenses with the rack and cog system in favour of connecting drive wheels with tools and crank pins.
- **1825** Stephenson's LOCOMOTION pulls 69 tons from Shildon to Stockton at the opening of the Stockton and Darlington Railway.
- **1829** George Stephenson's ROCKET wins the RAINHILL TRIALS.
- **1830** PHOENIX is the first engine with a smoke box is built by Stephenson & Co. for the Liverpool and Manchester Railway.
- Edward BURY's engine, the 0–4–0 LIVERPOOL is the first to have a bar frame and haycock firebox.
- PLANET is built by Stephenson & Co. for the Liverpool and Manchester Railway. NORTHUMBRIAN is built around the same time.
- **1834** Stephenson & Co. produce the PATENTEE. The Patentee is a natural development of the technology used for Planet, with the addition of an extra pair of rear wheels and the omission of wheel flanges.
- **1837** The LION is built by Todd, Kitson and Laird (Leeds).
- The North Star and Firefly are built by Stephenson & Co. to the Patentee design for the broad gauge GREAT WESTERN RAILWAY.

- **1846** The Iron Duke and the Great Western designed by Daniel Gooch for the Great Western Railway.
- David Joy and John Fenton design the Jenny Lind
- **1848** The 6–2–0 Liverpool is built by Thomas Crampton for the London and North Western Railway. It is the first standard gauge engine to match the speed of the GWR broad-gauge engines.
- **1861** J. G. McConnell builds the first of his Bloomers.
- **1870** Patrick Stirling produces his 4–2–2 engine No.1 (popularly known as the Stirling Single) for the Great Northern Railway.
- **1882–4** Anatole Mallet patents the compound locomotive. Francis Webb, superintendent with the London and North Western Railway, adopted and developed this principle with his own compound engine
- **1885** The Philadelphia and Reading Railway converts a narrow-gauge railway from Camden to Atlantic City with the intention of turning Atlantic City into a holiday resort for the citizens of Philadelphia. By 1890, business is booming to such an extent that additional carriages have to be employed and the extra load proves too much for the 4–4–0 Mother Hubbard class engine in use. This problem is solved by the development of a bigger boilered 4–4–2 engine, which is gradually improved upon until it is capable of regularly pulling 183 tons from Camden to Atlantic City. Thereafter, all 4–4–2 engines come to be known world-wide as Atlantics after their original destination.
- **1890s** Around this time demands for bigger and faster engines to pull ever-increasing loads of freight and passengers lead to the emergence of even bigger locomotives. In the closing years of the 19th century, several railways (notably those in Scotland) produce engines capable of coping with the increased demand.

steam locomotives

- **1894** David Jones produces 4–6–0 goods engines for the Highland railway.
- **1896** Mackintosh introduces the *Dunalastair* 4–4–0 class to the Caledonian Railway. This has bigger boilers than any previously seen.
- **1899** Aspinall's 4–4–2 Atlantic for the Lancashire and Yorkshire Railway is the first to be fitted with a SUPERHEATER.
- **1902** The 4–6–2 Pacific series is built for the Missouri and Pacific Railway company.
- **1907** George Churchward introduces his Star class 4–6–0. In **1908** these are fitted with superheaters and are, thereafter, unrivalled for power and economy in Britain.
- **1922** Collett (Churchward's successor at the GWR) develops the highly successful Castle class of 4–6–0.
- **1923** At this time, both Gresley and Stanier were working on 4–6–2 Pacific locomotives are introduced, so called because of the series built in 1922 for the Missouri Pacific Railway Co. The Atlantic and Pacific classes represented the last enlargements to locomotives engaged in passenger work.
- **1929–33** GWR's Cheltenham Flyer (a Castle 4–6–0) becomes the world's fastest train in daily use.
- **1930s** The Class A3 Pacific is introduced, using the long-lap valve gear principle (developed by Churchward) along with improved superheating.
- **1932** Dr Rudolph DIESEL's prototype diesel-electric streamliner is unveiled by the German Reichsbahn.
- **1934** GRESLEY's No. 4472 Flying Scotsman achieves 100mph on rail for the first time in Britain.
- **1935** Gresley's SILVER LINK becomes London and North Eastern Railway's first high speed train. Gresley adapts much of CHAPÉLON's theory for his design, although is yet to use the KYLCHAP EXHAUST SYSTEM.
- **1937** The CORONATION SCOT (STANIER) achieves a new British

speed record of 114mph (183km/h), narrowly avoiding a disastrous accident.
- **1938** Gresley's later A4 Pacifics are fitted with the KYLCHAP EXHAUST SYSTEM, most notably the famous MALLARD. Mallard achieved a staggering 126mph (203km/h), a feat never surpassed by a steam engine.
- **1939** The 6234 DUCHESS OF ABERCORN successfully hauls 610 tons up the punishing Beattock bank without falling below 31mph (50km/h).
- **1941** The US Union Pacific Railway introduces its 'big boys'; 345 ton 4-8-8-4 engines. These are designed to haul gargantuan freight loads over the Wasatch Mountains. They are later used to transport troops during World War Two.
- Oliver BULLEID produces the Merchant Navy class of Pacific for the Southern railway.
- **1945** Bulleid's West Country and Battle of Britain classes appear. His locomotives are partially streamlined passenger expresses, with some new features. The valve gear is contained within an oil bath and the wheels were redesigned to give added protection while negotiating curves. However from 1956 onwards when the engines are rebuilt, the streamlining is removed to give easier access to the working parts, and the chain-driven valve gear is abandoned as the oil bath is considered a fire hazard.
- **1951** R. A. Riddles' Britannia Pacifics are the only new major steam locomotive built after 1951. One of the later three-cylinder versions, No. 71000 DUKE OF GLOUCESTER, is the last steam express locomotive to be designed in Britain.

Stephenson, George (1781–1848)

Born in Wylam, near Newcastle upon Tyne, George Stephenson had little or no education in his youth. He worked in a colliery while learning to read and write, eventually working his way up to the position of engineman. The financial backing and confidence of the colliery owner, Lord Ravensworth, enabled Stephenson to build of his first steam engine in 1814. The engine, BLUCHER, was capable of pulling some eight loaded wagons—in total about 30 tons—at a speed of 4mph (6.5km/h). Like HEDLEY, Stephenson employed a series of gears to transmit power from engine to wheel. Blucher did not represent much of an improvement upon its predecessors, but it gave Stephenson the knowledge and the impetus to continue with his work.

His next engines employed TREVITHICK's device of venting exhaust steam through a narrow flue to intensify the heat of the fire. In addition, he hit upon the idea of mounting the cylinders on top of the boiler, thereby simplifying the drive to the wheels. Furthermore, he devised a system of rods and pins to couple driving wheels instead of cogs, a system which has been refined by successors, but never bettered.

Once the word of Stephenson's success had spread, the firm of Stephenson & Co. gathered orders from other railways for his new improved engines. The Quaker financier, Edward PEASE, who had secured an Act of Parliament in 1821 to build the STOCKTON AND DARLINGTON RAILWAY, appointed Stephenson as the line's engineer. On 17 September 1825, the railway was formally opened. The inaugural train, carrying a total load of 69 tons, was pulled by Stephenson's engine LOCOMOTION without hitch for 21 miles (34km)—it was the first-ever covered passenger coach.

In 1823, Stephenson had been appointed locomotive engineer to the projected LIVERPOOL AND MANCHESTER RAILWAY. After the company had been granted an Act of Parliament to build the railway, Stephenson was appointed Chief Engineer with responsibility for the entire railway—a formidable challenge for a self-taught man with no formal qualifications. However, time and again he confounded his critics by his ability to surmount the insurmountable problem. One famous example is his success in laying track across Chat Moss, a notoriously boggy area. Clearly, this appointment placed heavy demands on Stephenson and in 1827, his son Robert took charge of the Newcastle building works.

Despite Stephenson's reputation and his undisputed genius, the directors of the Liverpool and Manchester Railway still had little confidence in the reliability of steam traction, and were inclined to opt for stationary steam engines placed at intervals along the line providing rope haulage for wagonloads. Naturally, the Stephensons were horrified at their attitude, and agreed to take part in the RAINHILL TRIALS with other engine builders with the intention of demonstrating the reliability of steam locomotion. The success of Stephenson's engine, ROCKET, in these trials ensured that any doubts the directors had were eradicated and they ordered four more for the opening of the railway.

Stephenson, Robert (1803–59)

Robert was the son of George Stephenson, one of the best-known pioneering railway engineers, who became an outstanding engineer in his own right. Unlike his father, who was largely self-taught, Robert received a first-class education which enabled him to take charge of the family locomotive and engineering works in 1823. However, Robert wished to widen his experience and took off to Colombia, in America, for a three-year mining appointment, and a new company was set up on 1 January 1825 which established the Stephensons and their partners as railway engineers rather than builders of locomotives only.

Upon Robert's return, he became involved in the famous RAINHILL TRIALS. In 1833, he became chief engineer on the London and Birmingham Railway. However, Robert is probably best known for his bridges, the most famous of which are at Conwy, Menai Strait and Montreal, and the High Level bridge at Newcastle.

Stirling, Patrick (1820–95)

A Scottish mechanical engineer, Stirling was initially apprenticed to the Dundee Foundry before he gained experience in other engineering works. In 1853, he began work as locomotive superintendent of the Glasgow and South Western Railway. In 1866 he was appointed by the Great Northern Railway where he produced the STIRLING SINGLE engine.

Stirling Single

The Stirling Single locomotives were produced by Patrick STIRLING for the Great Northern Railway from 1870. The Single was characterized by an enormous driving wheel of 2438mm in diameter. It set a trend for the late-19th century by using a leading BOGIE and outside CYLINDERS. The Stirling Single also set records for speeds of up to 86mph (138km/h).

Stockton and Darlington Railway

The Stockton and Darlington Railway opened on 27 September 1825 and has the distinction of being the first public railway to adopt steam traction at the outset. Initially, its locomotives were used only to haul goods trains, and were not used for passengers until 1833.

superheater

The superheater was invented by the German designer and engineer Wilhelm SCHMIDT and was first used in 1898. It worked by raising the steam temperature before it went on to the CYLINDERS, thereby raising the steam pressure and therefore the efficiency of the engine. Some of the flue tubes within the BOILER are enlarged to accommodate the elements of the superheater. These elements effectively dry the steam further before sending which travels towards the FIREBOX and back before being sent on to the cylinders. Within ten years of its introduction, the superheater was being incorporated into the design of most large locomotives worldwide.

Surrey Iron Railway

The Surrey Iron Railway was the first public railway (incorporated in 1801) to be approved by parliament. It ran from Wandsworth to Croydon and opened on 26 July 1803. It connected to the Croydon, Merstham and Godstone Railway.

Swedish railways

Sweden's first railway was opened in 1849. This was a horse-operated narrow-gauge line from Frykstad to Lyckan. In March 1856, the first public railway opened on 1435mm GAUGE track and ran from Nora to Ervalia. The early lines were publicly owned, but as the system grew, the main trunk lines were absorbed into state ownership, whilst private enterprise retained control over many of the branch lines.

Swedish State railways (SJ—Svenska Statens Jørnvøgar) were the first in Europe to separate railway operation from infrastructure. Bankverket (the track authority) now extracts a toll from train operators for the use of the track. Bankverket operates 6905 miles (11,119km), the majority which 1435mm gauge and the rest 891mm gauge.

Sykes, William Robert (1749–1838)

Sykes began his career with the London, Brighton and South Coast Railway where he introduced track circuiting in 1864. Whilst working for the London, Chatham and Dover railway, he invented the 'lock and block' system of signalling which he patented in 1875. It aimed to further reduce opportunity for human error in the interlocking system by extending it to govern the block instrument as well as the signals and points. However, the company was reluctant to install this safety measure and only after strong encouragement from the Board of Trade was the Victoria to Dover line equipped with it. He founded the Sykes Interlocking Signal System Co. in 1899.

T

tank engines
The tank engine was developed for light passenger and suburban work for which a locomotive was required to be extremely manoeuvrable and fairly fast. Unlike tender engines, tank engines carried their own water in tanks and their coal in a bunker. The main advantage of this was that the engine moved in either direction, which removed the awkward manoeuvring process required to turn it around.

Tank engines developed a reputation for unreliability, and large tank engines in particular were used less and less for passenger express work. None the less, they did have their devotees and seemed to work perfectly well in some locations. The railways of North Wales, for instance, enthusiastically adopted the tank engine for passenger and FREIGHT use alike.

There are three main types of tank engine, classified by the positioning of the tanks. Side tank engines had their tanks on the main frame member at either side of the boiler. Pannier tank engines had tanks supported by the BOILER, while those on the saddle tank engine straddled the boiler.

tender
Locomotives used for long-distance service had a separate truck known as a tender situated behind the cab to carry water and coal. The tender consisted basically of a water tank and a coal

space, and had a capacity of between 2,500 and 5,000 gallons of water and approximately four to eight tons of coal.

TGV/ Trains a Grands Vitesse
French high-speed trains.

third rail
A rail supplying the current to electric trains, usually situated slightly above and to one side of the running rails. The current is collected by a 'shoe' on the locomotive.

tracks
For as long as man has required to shift goods or people in wagons or trucks, he has devised some sort of track to prevent his wheels disappearing into ruts of mud wherever a particular route is used repeatedly. The Greeks and Romans surmounted this problem to some extent by using wagonways of grooved stone, whilst wooden railways were deployed in European mines from the 1700s. The wooden railways were almost adequate as long as the wagons were pushed or pulled by man or horse, but with the advent of the STEAM LOCOMOTIVE something rather more substantial was required.

One of the earliest attempts at making a railway out of iron was the plateway, which was a vast improvement on wooden rails in terms of stability and durability. It had FLANGEd cast-iron rails supported by stone SLEEPERS, but cast-iron is brittle and fractures easily. Furthermore, as the volume of rail traffic increased, it became imperative that trains could be moved easily from one track to another. This was best done by merging two lines together at one point, or switch—something for which the plateway was not well suited.

Railway engineers experimented with various different solutions to the problem, including a fish-belly rail with a deeper centre section to provide extra strength. Plateways were finally abandoned in the 1820s in favour of smooth-edged rails made of wrought iron which was less brittle than cast-iron, and therefore much better suited to steam traction. Stone was replaced by wood for sleepers, and eventually the Midland Railway introduced steel rails in 1857. The SLEEPERS sat snugly on a base of stone chip BALLAST which effectively provided both stability and drainage.

From 1857, the appearance of the track was quite similar to that which is used today, but there are several important differences. Sleepers are now made of steel or concrete, and the section of the rail has changed from the bull-head of the 1870s to the modern flat-bottomed design adopted in the 1950s. On longer sections of track unimpeded by points, rails are laid in single welded pre-stressed lengths of up to 1610 metres (1 mile). Pre-stressing ameliorates the effects on the metal of any sudden rise and fall in temperature, as do sliding expansion joints. The rails transmit a weak electrical current as part of the signalling system known as track circuiting (*see* SIGNALLING) and are therefore required to be insulated from sleepers and fastenings.

First rate maintenance is vital to the safe running of the railway. Gangs of platelayers regularly inspect all lines to check the gauge is correct, to monitor the condition of the BALLAST, SLEEPERS and rails, and also to clear any obstacles or vegetation from the line.

train
The term is given to any vehicle or series of vehicles on wheels which is either self-propelled or pulled by a locomotive.

tram
Any vehicle employed on a TRAMWAY or tramroad.

tramway
Since the mid-19th century, tramway has been the name given

to a system of passenger transport (although goods are occasionally carried) on a track laid in an urban or suburban area. The tracks are usually laid in the centre of the street. Since the final years of the 19th century, most urban tramways have been powered by electricity by means of overhead cables from which the current is collected via a pantograph or other device on the roof of the tram.

Trevithick, Richard (1771–1833)
The first self-propelled steam engine was built in 1800–1 by Richard Trevithick, and was intended for use on the road. Although its success was limited due to its lack of suspension and the bumpiness of the roads, he was sufficiently encouraged to design and build a railway locomotive at Coalbrookdale in Shropshire. Although it is unclear as to whether or not this engine ever ran, the owner of Pendarren ironworks in South Wales was confident enough to ask Trevithich for an engine to run on the tramway at his Merthyr Tydfil works in 1804. The engine was built, and Trevithick won a bet with a friend that his engine could pull 40 tons. However, the plate rails which were in use at the time did not have the strength to support the weight of the engine. The project was abandoned and the engine had its wheels removed and was retained to drive machinery.

Trevithick had two further attempts to drum up commercial interest in his locomotives. The third engine, built at Gateshead in 1805, was the first to employ flanged wheels. Another was demonstrated in London on a circular track in Euston Square in 1808. This engine (known as CATCH ME WHO CAN) successfully reached a speed of 11.5mph (19km/h) whilst pulling a coach containing passengers. However, even this revolutionary feat of innovation failed to generate any commercial enthusiasm and Trevithick concentrated his efforts thereafter on stationary steam engines.

Trevithick had contributed some knowledge which was to prove vital to the future development of the steam engine. He demonstrated that it was possible for a smooth iron wheel to grip sufficiently on a smooth iron rail to pull a heavy load. He established that the heating area between the fire and water had to be sufficient to produce the requisite amount of steam; that the exhaust system could be used to heat the water before pumping it into the boiler and that if the exhaust is directed up the chimney it has the effect of drawing the fire up and making it burn brightly.

Sadly, Trevithick died penniless in London. Other engineers were slow to take up his ideas, although it may be that they had not heard of his pioneering work.

tube

The popular name for the London Underground rail system (*see* UNDERGROUND RAILWAYS).

Tyer, Edward (1830–1912)

Edward Tyer was a British signalling engineer responsible for many improvements to the rail system. In 1853, he devised a way of registering automatically to the signalman the arrival of a train in his block. He then invented a lock-and-key commutator to improve communications between signalmen. (*See also* SIGNALLING.)

U

Ukrainian Railways

Ukrainian Railways was created in 1991 and comprises six of the old USSR system's regions. UZ (Ukrainia Zalinitza) operates 14,498 miles (23,346km) of 1524mm track.

underground railways

The railways' success in the 19th century brought greater numbers of people and businesses to large cities, resulting in ever increasing congestion on the streets. Eventually, a House of Commons Select Committee recommended the building of an underground railway to connect the main line stations. This was in 1855, and in 1863, the Metropolitan built opened its first line connecting Paddington and Farringdon Street. The tunnel was built using the method whereby a trench was dug and then covered to form a tunnel—known as cut and cover. Steam trains were used, which created huge problems in terms of the air quality in the tunnels. Special tank engines were used which condensed water in the tanks so that it could be used again thereby cutting down on steam emissions, but exhaust smoke had nowhere to go but into the tunnel itself.

However, despite these technical problems, the system—known as the tube—proved to be much more convenient and faster than road travel. Many cities, including New York and Paris, have followed London's example and built their own underground systems as they became aware of the benefits. Nowadays, of course, most underground systems use electric trains which has eliminated the problems of poor air quality and fumes in the tunnels.

V

Volk, Magnus (1851–1937)

Magnus Volk was the engineer responsible for the first electric railway in this country—the Electric Railway in Brighton. He also designed the Brighton and Rottingdean Seashore Electric Tramway (1896–1901).

W

Walschaerts, Egide (1820–1901)
Walschaerts was the Belgian engineer who invented the valve gear bearing his name. Such was its success that it became the most widely used in the history of the steam traction engine.

Watt, James (1736–1819)
Scottish engineer and inventor whose work on steam engines was to have a profound influence on the development of steam locomotion. He was trained as a maker of mathematical instruments and worked as a surveyor on canals before he became interested in the potential of steam power, around 1759.

While involved in the repair of a steam pumping engine, he devised several improvements to the design. Watts was thus inspired to develop his own designs in partnership with Matthew Boulton (1728–1809), at the Soho Engineering Works outside Birmingham. His first commercial steam pumping engine was produced in 1775 and was patented seven years later. The improvements he had made to the steam engine led to the use of steam power in industry. His work also described the principles of steam locomotion and he gave his name to the unit of power, the watt, and was the first person to use the unit horsepower.

Webb, Francis (1836-1906)
Webb was the engineer superintendent on the LONDON AND NORTH WESTERN RAILWAY who adopted MALLET'S compound engine principles and employed them extensively on his own engines. Webb's compound engines sadly never achieved the required reliability, and they were deemed too costly to build, and too complex to drive and maintain in comparison with simple engines.

Westinghouse, George (1846–1914)
Westinghouse was the designer of the famous Westinghouse non-automatic 'straight air' brake, patented in 1868. He later developed an automatic brake. Although much refined, the original principle behind Westinghouse's air brake remains unchanged today.

Whistler, George Washington (1800–1849)
Whistler was one of the USA's railway pioneers who was responsible for the laying out of several of America's earliest railways.

Whyte's notation
As engine types became larger and more varied and three-axled formations were increasingly enlarged upon, Whyte's notation was developed in order to classify locomotives more easily. As most locomotives have a combination of driving wheels and smaller trailing (or BOGIE) wheels, a system of three numbers evolved. For example, the ROCKET design would use the notation 0–2–2 which would indicate 2 small leading wheels, followed by 2 driving wheels, followed by 2 small trailing wheels. In Europe, the axles were labelled rather than the wheels. Therefore, the configuration for Rocket would be 0–1–1.

Z

Zürich to Baden Railway
The Zürich to Baden, inaugurated on 9 August 1847, was the first railway to open entirely in Switzerland. (The BASEL TO ST LOUIS terminated at St Louis in France.)

Chronology of Rail and Steam

1758

Britain's first Railway Act authorizes the opening of the Middleton Railway, Leeds.

1801

The first public railway sanctioned by Parliament, the Surrey Iron Railway, is incorporated on 21 May.

1803

Richard Trevithick builds his first steam locomotive for the Coalbrookdale Ironworks in Shropshire.

1804

Trevithick's second steam locomotive successfully pulls a load of 70 men, ten tons of iron and an extra five wagons on 'L' section rails at the Pen-y-Darren Ironworks in South Wales on 22 February.

On 29 June the Oystermouth Railway Company is incorporated and commences construction of a railway between Swansea and Mumbles.

1805

Trevithick's third locomotive is completed at Gateshead and was the first locomotive to use flanged wheels. Unfortunately, the rails are unable to bear the weight of the locomotive.

1806

The short 'D' patterned slide valve is invented by Matthew Murray at Leeds.

Chronology of Rail and Steam

1808
The Kilmarnock and Troon Railway is incorporated on 27 May, becoming the first real railway in Scotland.

1811
John Blenkinsop obtains a patent for his steam locomotive which uses the toothed wheel and rack system.

1812
On 12 August, Matthew Murray's toothed-wheel and rack-type steam locomotive begins service on the Middleton Railway, Leeds, and becomes the first locomotive to be hailed as a commercial success.

James Fenton introduces his spring-loaded safety valve.

William Hedley carries out experiments at Wylam to demonstrate that smooth wheels can provide the necessary adhesion to the track, thereby obviating the toothed wheel and rack system.

1813
Hedley builds his first locomotive, the Grasshopper, at Wylam. It had four flanged wheels, two vertical cylinders which drove the wheels by means of levers and connecting rods and a central jack-shaft.

William Brunton (1777-1851) patents a locomotive which was propelled by a pair of legs situated at the rear.

1814
On 25 July, George Stephenson completes his first locomotive, the Blucher, at Killingworth.

1815
At Killingworth, Stephenson and Ralph Dodds patent a locomotive with directly-driven wheels coupled by chains.

1816
George Stephenson and Nicholas Wood (1795-1865) introduce

their loose eccentric valve gear, later to be used on Rocket and Planet.

1818
Charles Carmichael introduces his single fixed eccentric valve gear.

1823
The St Etienne-Andrézieux Railway receives its concession on 26 February to become the first railway in France.

1825
The Stockton and Darlington Railway opens on 27 September. George Stephenson's Locomotion, the first to use wheels coupled by rods, successfully hauls a train loaded with passengers and coal.

1826
The Liverpool and Manchester Railway is incorporated (5 May). Expansion valve gear, the multi-jet blast pipe and the fusible plug are all invented by Sir Goldsworthy Gurney (1793-1875).

1827
Hackworth's locomotive, Royal George, is built at Shildon, County Durham. It is the first locomotive to have its wheels driven directly by the cylinders, and also the first ever six-coupled locomotive.
Marc Séguin patents the multi-tubular boiler.
The Baltimore and Ohio Railroad is incorporated on 5 May.
Austro-Hungary's first railway opens from Budweis to Trojanov on 7 September.

1828
George Stephenson's Lancashire Witch is delivered to the Bolton and Leigh Railway, which opens on 1 August.
St Etienne-Andrézieux opens officially on 1 October.

Chronology of Rail and Steam

1829

Stephenson's Rocket wins the Rainhill Trials, thus establishing the suitability of steam locomotives for the railways.

1830

The Canterbury and Whitstable Railway opens using steam traction (3 May).

The Baltimore and Ohio Railroad opens its first section from Baltimore to Ellicot's Mills in Maryland on 24 May.

On 15 September, the Liverpool and Manchester Railway becomes Britain's first 'modern' main line railway.

Stephenson builds Phoenix, the first ever locomotive to have a smokebox.

Edward Bury's 0-4-0 Liverpool introduces the bar frame and haycock firebox. It also one of the earliest engines with inside cylinders under the firebox driving a cranked axle.

Stephenson builds his 2-2-0 Planet for the Liverpool and Manchester Railway with a similar cylinder arrangement to that of Bury's Liverpool. It was also the first locomotive to have outside bearings and 'sandwich' frames.

1831

Rothwell Hick and Rothwell of Bolton build a locomotive which is the first to have outside cylinders directly attached to the frame.

Michael Faraday (1791-1867) makes a discovery which will eventually lead to the invention of the dynamo—that of magnetic induction.

1832

Stephenson experiments with piston valves and introduces 'petticoat blast pipe.'

Horatio Allen builds the first ever articulated locomotive for the South Carolina Railroad.

1833

Stephenson's Patentee becomes the first locomotive to have a steam brake.

J & C Carmichael build a locomotive for the Dundee and Newtyle railway which is the first in Britain to have a bogie.

Joseph Saxton demonstrates a prototype rotative dynamo in June at Cambridge.

1834

The first railway amalgamation Act joins the Wigan Branch and the Wigan and Preston Railway which become the North Union Railway, Lancashire.

On 17 December, Ireland's first railway (from Dublin to Dun Laoghaire) opens.

The first cylindrical smokebox is used in America.

Hiram Strait patents his balanced slide valve in New York.

1835

Blacksmith Thomas Davenport makes a model electric railway in Vermont, USA.

Germany's first railway, the Ludwigsbahn, opens on 7 December between Nuremberg and Furth, using Stephenson's locomotive Der Adler.

1836

London's first railway opens—a section of the London and Greenwich Railway between Spa Road and Deptford.

Sandboxes are fitted to locomotives in the USA for the first time.

The Welsh Ffestiniog Railway opens to carry slate on 20 April. It is the first narrow gauge railway in the world (600mm), although steam traction is not used until 1863.

Canada's first steam railway, the Champlain and St Lawrence opens between Laprairie and St John on 21 July, using Robert Stephenson's locomotive, Dorchester.

Chronology of Rail and Steam

Russia's first railway opens on 9 October between Tsarskoe Selo and Pavlovsk, using horse traction.

1837

Britain's first trunk railway, the Grand Junction, opens on 4 July between Birmingham and Warrington, connecting the Liverpool and Manchester Railway with the London and Birmingham.

The USA's first 4–4–0 (incorporating inside cylinders) is built in Philadelphia.

1838

The Kaiser Ferdinand Nordbahn opens between Vienna and Florisdorf and Deutsch Wagram on 6 January, making it the first railway situated entirely in (modern) Austria.

The Great Western Railway opens its first section from London to Maidenhead on 4 June.

The London and Birmingham Railway is completed on 17 September, making it the first main line to London.

John Gray of the Liverpool and Manchester Railway is the first to use Hiram Strait's balanced slide valve in this country.

1839

The Netherlands' first railway opens between Amsterdam and Haarlem on 24 September.

Italy's first Railway, the Naples to Portici opens on 4 October.

John Gray first uses expansion valve gear on a locomotive on the North Midland Railway.

R & W Hawthorn introduce locomotive superheating to a locomotive at Newcastle upon Tyne.

Norris of Philadelphia produces the first American 'classic' 4-4-0.

1840

John Gray introduces long-travel valves to the Hull and Selby Railway, affording greater cylinder efficiency.

1841

Experiments are conducted with the firebox brick arch, in an attempt to produce smokeless coal combustion.

Ross Winans builds the first 0-8-0 in Baltimore, USA.

Robert Stephenson uses sanding gear on a British locomotive for the first time.

The Manchester and Leeds Railway opens on 1 March, making it the first to cross the Pennines.

1842

The Edinburgh and Glasgow Railway opens on 1 March.

Robert Davidson succeeds in running a 5 tonne battery-driven electric locomotive on the Edinburgh and Glasgow Railway at 4mph/6.5kmh.

1843

Howe invents link motion, which is first used on Robert Stephenson's locomotives on the North Midland Railway and becomes known as Stationary Link Motion.

Daniel Gooch uses Stationary Link motion on the Great Western Railway. John Veret (1812–1900), Gooch's brother does likewise on the London and South Western.

1844

Switzerland's first railway opens on 15 June. It runs from Basel to St Louis in France.

Egide Walschaerts invents his valve gear in Belgium.

James Nasmyth (1808–90) invents the pneumatic brake.

1845

Scinz proposes the the replacement of the mercurial gauge by the dial pressure.

The London and Birmingham Railway becomes the first to carry out balancing of locomotive driving wheels.

Chronology of Rail and Steam

1846

Hungary opens its first railway from Pest to Vacz on 15 July.

The Gauge Act receives Royal Assent on 18 August.

Britain is at the height of the 'Railway mania' with 273 railway bills receiving Royal Assent in this year alone.

Stephenson & Co. produce the first three-cylinder locomotive for the Newcastle and North Berwick Railway.

In the USA, the Norris Bros. of Philadelphia build the first 4-6-0 locomotive for the Philadelphia and Reading railroad.

1847

The Copenhagen-Roskilde railway opens on 26 June, the first in modern Denmark.

The first railway entirely within Switzerland, the Zürich-Baden Railway, opens on 9 August.

1848

The Caledonian Railway opens from Carlisle to Edinburgh and Glasgow on 15 February.

Spain's first railway, from Barcelona to Mataro, opens on 28 October.

South America's first railway opens on 3 November and runs from Georgetown to Plaisance (now in Guyana).

The Boston and Providence Railroad is the first in the USA to use a steam brake on a locomotive.

1849

Eltham Rogers introduces the variable cut-off valve gear in Cleveland, Ohio, USA.

1850

The Scottish North Eastern Railway completes the 'West Coast Route' from London to Aberdeen via Perth on 1 April.

The opening of the Great Northern Railway between Warrington Junction, Peterborough and London completes the

East Coast Route (between London, Edinburgh and Glasgow) on 7 August. East coast trains had used a temporary bridge in Berwick-upon-Tweed until the Royal Borders Bridge was opened on 29 August.

Compounding of cylinders is tried and patented for the first time by engineer James Samuel of the Eastern Counties Railway. It had, however, been invented by John Nicholson of the same railway.

Ramsbottom introduces the double-beat regulator valve on the London and North Western Railway.

1851

First train services run on the Moscow to St Petersburg railway on 1 November.

Alfred Krupp (1812–87) of Germany introduces steel locomotive tyres, which proved to be much more durable than iron tyres.

1852

Edward Bury introduces his drop grate for ease of fire cleaning.

A smokebox superheater is introduced on the London and North Eastern Railway by J. E. McConnell.

1853

India's first railway, The Great Indian Peninsula Railway Company's Bombay to Thana line, opens on 18 April.

1854

Brazil's first railway, from Maua to the Petropolis Serra, opens on 30 April.

Australia's first public freight and passenger railway opens on 18 May, powered by horse traction.

Norway's first railway opens on 1 September from Christiana (now Oslo) to Edsvoll.

Australia's first steam-powered railway opened on 12 September between Melbourne and Port Melbourne.

Chronology of Rail and Steam

1855

J. H. Beattie carries out first trial of feed-water heater on the London and South Western Railway.

Alexander Allan invents straight-link motion valve gear which is used on Scottish Central Railway locomotives.

1856

Africa's first railway from Alexandra to Cairo opens in January.

The first through trains run from Montreal to Toronto on Canada's Grand trunk railway.

Portugal's first railway, the Lisbon to Corregado, opens on 28 October.

Swedish State Railways open first sections between Gothenberg and Jonsered and Lund and Malmo on 1 December.

John Saxby patents interlocking of points and signals.

The London and North Western Railway's John Ramsbottom introduces the screw reverser, the duplex safety valve and the displacement lubricator.

1857

Argentina's first railway opens–the Parque to Floresta– on 30 August.

1858

G. K. Douglas first uses the firehole deflector plate on the Birkenhead, Lancashire and Cheshire Junction Railway.

1859

The brick arch and firehole deflector plate are used together for the first time on a Midland Railway locomotive. The combination is devised by Matthew Kirtley's assistant, Charles Markham.

Henri Giffard (1825–82) invents the steam injector.

1860

South Africa's first railway, from Durban to Natal, opens on 26 June.

Chronology of Rail and Steam

William Sellers introduces the steam injector to the USA.

Alexander Allan experiments with a steel locomotive firebox on the Scottish Central Railway, but copper remains the preferred boiler construction material in Britain and Europe.

William Bouch produces the first 4-4-0 for the Stockton and Darlington Railway.

Canada's Hamilton works produces the first steel boiler.

1861
Pakistan's first railway, from Karachi to Kotri, opens on 13 May.

1862
George Tosh introduces Britain's first steel boilers on the Maryport and Carlisle Railway.

1863
London's Metropolitan Railway opens on January 10th to become the first city underground service and runs from Bishop's Road to Farringdon Street.

New Zealand opens its first steam-powered railway on 1 December from Christchurch to Ferrymead.

W. B. Adams' radial axlebox is used for the first time on some tank engines belonging to the St Helen's Railway, Lancashire.

1864
Alfred Belpaire's square firebox is used for the first time on Belgian State Railways.

Robert Fairlie patents his double-bogie articulated locomotive.

1865
Ceylon's (now Sri Lanka) first railway opens from Colombo to Ambepussa on 2 October.

1866
The Troy and Boston Railroad's George W. Richardson patents the 'pop' safety valve.

Chronology of Rail and Steam

1867
The Lehigh Railroad, USA, introduces the first 2-10-0 locomotive.

1869
The first North American trans-continental railway is completed at Promontory, Utah. This was achieved by joining the Central Pacific and the Union Pacific Railroads.

Romania opens its first railroad, from Bucharest to Giurgiu, on 19 October.

1871
Thomas Wheatley his 4-4-0 locomotive with inside cylinders on the North British Railway.

Steel and McInnes use a compressed air-brake for the first time on the Caledonian Railway.

1872
Japan's first railway, from Yokohama to Shinagawa, opens on 12 June. By 14 October, the next section to Tokyo had been completed.

1873
Belgium's Zénobe Gramme (1826-1901) invents the DC commutator motor.

1874
J. Y. Smith introduces the non-automatic vacuum brake on the North Eastern Railway.

T. Adams' pop safety valve is used on a British locomotive for the first time.

William Stroudley uses a speed indicator on the Brighton and South Coast Railway.

James Stirling (1808-83) uses a steam reversing gear for the first time on the Glasgow and South Western Railway.

William Mason first uses Egide Walschaerts' valve gear on a Boston, Clinton and Fitchburg Railroad-owned locomotive.

1876

Francis Webb introduces the hydraulic brake on the London and North Western Railway.

Anatole Mallets first compound locomotive is built in France.

Davies and Metcalfe develop an exhaust-steam injector.

1877

John E. Wootten (1822-1898) invents a wide firebox during his time as general manager of the Philadelphia and Reading Railroad, USA.

1878

Thomas Bouch's bridge over the River Tay opens on 1 June. The bridge was to collapse during a gale in December of the following year whilst a train crossed.

James Gresham (1836-1914) invents the automatic vacuum brake.

William Adams designs Britain's first 2-6-0s for the Great Eastern Railway.

1879

David Joy's radial valve gear is first tested on a Bury 0-4-0 belonging to the Furness Railway.

Werner von Siemens demonstrates his electric railway at the Berlin Trades Exhibition. It successfully pulled 30 passengers and was the world's first practical electric railway.

1880

China builds its first permanent 1435mm gauge railway between Tongskan and Hsukuchuang.

Thomas Edison begins experimenting with electric railways in New Jersey.

Chronology of Rail and Steam

1881

The world's first electric railway opens at Lichtefelde, Berlin on 12 May. It succeeded in hauling a load of 26 passengers at a speed of 48kph (30mph).

1883

The Urquhart system is employed regularly to use oil as fuel for the Russian South Eastern Railway.

Magnus Volk opens his Electric Railway at Brighton on 4 August.

Ireland's Portrush to Giant's Causeway Tramway opens on 28 September, making it the first railway powered by hydro-electricity.

Leo Daft builds the Ampère, the first electric locomotive for the standard gauge, to run on the Saratoga and Mount MacGregor Railroad in the USA.

1884

London's Inner Circle (part of the Metropolitan and District Railways) is completed.

Mallet patents his Mallet-type articulated locomotive.

1885

The first transcontinental railway in Canada, the Canadian Pacific, is completed on 7 November.

1886

Webb introduces steel plate frames on the London and North Western Railway.

0-8-0 locomotives are used for the first time in Britain on the Barry Railway, South Wales.

The Midland Railway introduces steam sanding gear, designed by James Gresham and Francis Holt.

The Vulcan Iron Works, Pennsylvania build the first 4-6-2 locomotive.

1887
Oil used as locomotive fuel for the first time in Britain on the GER and in the US on the Pennsylvania Railroad.

1888
The Vulcan Iron works in the USA builds the first Strong-designed 4-4-2 locomotive for the Lehigh Valley Railroad. The 4-4-2 type was later to become better known as the Atlantic.

The Serbian Nikola Tesla (1856-1943) invents the AC electric motor in the USA.

1889
The Regulation of Railways Act receives Royal Assent on 30 August. The Act makes it a legal requirement for railways to use the block signalling system, signal and point interlocking and continuous automatic brakes on passenger trains.

1890
The world's biggest cantilever railway bridge over the Firth of Forth near Edinburgh opens on 4 March.

The first underground railway to be powered by electric, the City and South London Railway, opens on 18 December. Mather and Platt, of Salford, supplied the electric four-wheeled locomotives.

1892
Britain's first 0-8-0 locomotive with inside cylinders is built at Crewe. It is designed by Francis Webb.

1893
The world's first elevated electric city railway, the Liverpool Overhead Railway, opens on 6 March.

1894
Designer David Jones introduces Britain's first 4-6-0 locomotive on the Highland Railway.

Chronology of Rail and Steam

1895

The Great Western Railway begins to use long smokeboxes, as favoured in America, although they have been tried some years previously by the Great Eastern and Mersey Railway and the Glasgow and South Western Railway.

The New York, New Haven and Hartford Railroad opens the first electric train service.

The Baltimore and Ohio Railroad introduce electric freight locomotives in August.

The Chicago Overhead Railway introduces electric trains.

1897

James Manson introduces Britain's first four-cylinder simple-expansion locomotive, 4-4-0 No 11, to the Glasgow and South Western Railway.

The Chicago South Side Elevated Railway uses electric trains without locomotives employing Julian Sprague's system of multiple-unit control.

1898

Henry Ivatt designs Britain's first 4-4-2 Atlantic for the Great Northern Railway.

Dr Rudolph Diesel introduces the first diesel engine.

1899

Wilson Wordsell's (1850–1920) 4-6-0 passenger locomotive, the first in Britain, is built for the North Eastern Railway.

Sir John Aspinall fits a smokebox superheater to a Lancashire and Yorkshire Railway 4-4-2, making it Britain's first superheated locomotive.

Switzerland's Burgdorf-Thun Railway is the first to use an AC current system.

1900

Baldwin Locomotive Works, USA, produce the first 2-6-2 tender engine, which eventually gains the name Prairie as a result of its popularity on the lines of the mid-west.

1901
The superheater is used for the first time in North America.

The world's longest railway, the Trans-Siberian, opens on 3 November.

1902
The Great Northern Railway introduces the wide firebox on one of Ivatt's 4-4-2s.

James Holden builds Britain's first 0-10-0 for the Great Eastern Railway.

The Berlin Elevated Railway begins operating as an electric railway from the outset.

1903
The 2-10-2 type engine, Santa Fe, is introduced by the Atcheson, Topeka and Santa Fe Railroad, USA.

Churchward introduces Britain's first 2-8-0 on the Great Western Railway.

The electrification of the Mersey Railway is completed, making it the first British steam railway to convert to electricity. A third rail is used to provide the 600 V DC current.

1904
The North Eastern Railway uses the first section of electrification on Tyneside to provide the first electrified suburban service on 29 March. The Lancashire and Yorkshire followed suit on their Southport line, a part of which was opened on 5 April.

Switzerland's Seebach-Wettingen railway introduces a single-phase AC system.

1905
Lentz first applies his poppet valve gear to a German locomotive.

Chronology of Rail and Steam

The Pennsylvania Railroad fits its 2-8-2s with mechanical stokers.

The London 'Inner Circle' is officially electrified on 12 April, and its last steam train ran on 22 September. It uses a third rail supplying a 600 V DC current.

1906

Churchward of the Great Western Railway and George Hughes of the Lancashire and Yorkshire Railway use smoke-tube superheaters for the first time in Britain.

The 12-mile-long Simplon tunnel from Switzerland to Italy is completed and formally opened on 1 June.

1907

Herbert Garratt patents his articulated locomotive.

Switzerland's Misox Railway becomes the first in the world to use the 1500 V dc overhead system. This system was to become standard throughout the world.

1908

Britain's first Pacific 4-6-2 locomotive is built by the Great Western Railway at Swindon.

The world's first steam turbine locomotive is built at Milan. It is designed by Professor Belluzzo.

On 1 February, the Midland Railway introduces electric trains on the Morecambe-Heysham line with an experimental 6600 V single phase ac system at 25 Hz.

1910

The North British Locomotive Company builds a steam-turbine-electric locomotive designed by W. M. Ramsey and Sir Hugh Reid.

The metre-gauge Trans-Andine Railway opens from Los Andes in Chile to Mendoza in Argentina on 5 April.

1912-13
The North British Locomotive Company builds the first diesel locomotive.

1913
The first diesel rail car goes into operational service in Sweden. Switzerland's Rhaetian Railway electrifies its first section using 11 000 V $16^2/_3$ Hz.

1915
A double collision occurs at Quintinshill, north of Carlisle, as a result of signalling failure. More than 220 lives were lost, making it the worst railway disaster in Britain.

The 1500 V DC overhead system is introduced to Britain on the North Eastern Railway's Shildon to Newport line.

1916
The Manchester and Bury Railway introduces electric trains using a side contact third rail 1200 V DC system.

1917
Commonwealth Railways open the Trans-Australian railway on 22 October, incorporating the world's longest stretch of straight railway 478 kilometres (297 miles).

1920
The Caprotti valve gear is used for the first time on an Italian 2-6-0.

1921
The Railways Act decreeing the amalgamation of Britain's railway companies into four groups receives Royal Assent on 19 August.

1922
The Great Northern Railway produces a series of 4-6-2s.

1923

The American Locomotive Company builds the first diesel-electric locomotive to become a commercial success.

The British railway companies (123 in total) are amalgamated to form four groups: the London, Midland and Scottish, the Great Western, the Southern and the London and North Eastern.

1924

The London and North Eastern Railway experiments with diesel traction for the first time in Britain.

1925

German State Railways build the first 'main line' diesel-electric locomotives designed by George V. Lomonosoff (1876-1952).

1928

A former electric train belonging to the Lancashire and Yorkshire Railway is converted to become Britain's first diesel-electric train.

The London and North Eastern Railway begins operating the longest non-stop run in the world from London to Edinburgh on 1 May.

1929

Gresley designs an experimental 4-6-4 four-cylinder high-pressure compound locomotive for the London and North Eastern Railway.

The North British Locomotive company builds an experimental three-cylinder high-pressure compound 4-6-0 locomotive (Fury) for the London Midland and Scottish Railway.

1930

The London Underground installs the first mercury-arc rectifier on a British railway, a development which permitted the used of unmanned substations.

Chronology of Rail and Steam

1931

Britain's first diesel locomotive goes into regular service on the London Midland and Scottish Railway.

The Manchester South Junction and Altrincham becomes the first passenger railway in Britain to use a 1500 V DC overhead system.

1932

The Flying Hamburger runs between Berlin and Hamburg, achieving speeds of 100mph (161km/h), making it the world's first high-speed diesel train.

1933

The London, Midland and Scottish Railway introduces Stanier's 4-6-2 design locomotive.

The London to Brighton becomes Britain's first electrified main line, using the 660 V third rail system.

1934

The Chicago, Burlington and Quincy Railroad, USA, introduce the first stream-lined diesel-electric train.

1935

The London, Midland and Scottish builds a Stanier-designed 4-6-2 with direct-drive turbine.

Gresley's class 'A4' streamlined Pacifics, the first in Britain, are introduced by the London and North Eastern Railway.

1937

The London Midland and Scottish Railway introduces Stanier's streamlined 4-6-2s.

1938

The London Midland and Scottish builds the first streamlined diesel train in Britain.

Mallard achieves the world speed record (never broken by a

steam engine) for the London and North Eastern Railway on the Grantham to Peterborough run.

1939

General Motors, USA, produce their 'Electro-motive' diesel-electric freight locomotive. Its performance sealed the fate of the steam locomotive, with its ability to pull heavy loads over sustained periods up long steep gradients.

1941

The Brown Boveri Company of Baden produce the world's first gas-turbine-electric locomotive for Swiss Federal Railways.

1947

The London Midland and Scottish becomes the first British railway to operate diesel-electric locomotives on main lines.

The Transport Act laying out the conditions of the nationalisation of British road, canal and rail services receives Royal Assent on 6 August.

1948

The General Electric Company produces America's first gas-turbine-electric locomotives for the Union Pacific Railroad.

The rail network in Britain is nationalized on 1 January and becomes British Rail.

1949

Budd diesel railcars are introduced to North America.

1950

Brown Boveri gas-turbine-electric locomotives are introduced to Britain by British Rail's Western Region.

The Tal-y-llyn Railway in Wales becomes the first 'preserved' railway in the world in July.

The German 50 Hz Höllental line ends up in France as a result of World War Two. As a result of this, the French opt to install a similar 50 Hz system (25 kV) between Aix les Bains and La Roche-sur-Foron in the South Eastern Region.

1952

The first British-built gas-turbine-electric locomotive becomes operational on British Rail's Western Region in January.

112 people are killed as a result of a double collision on 8 October at Harrow. The disaster provides additional impetus for the provision of Automatic Warning system to all main lines.

1953

On the Lancaster to Heysham section of the old Midland Railway, British Rail carries out trials with 50 Hz 6600V electrification. The power cars use DC traction motors and mercury-arc rectifiers. Services commences on 17 August.

1954

British Rail introduces Diesel multiple unit trains.

The first 'all-electric' main line in Britain opens on 14 September. The line which ran from Manchester to Sheffield, is fully operational for both freight and passenger traffic using 1500 V dc via overhead cables.

1955

The English Electric Company produces the first of the diesel 'Deltics' at the Lancashire Vulcan Works.

France claims the world speed record with a 1500 V dc electric train.

British Railways introduces a sleeper service in June between London and Perth with the capacity to carry private motor cars on flat wagons to the rear of the train.

1956

British Rail takes the decision to adopt as standard the 25kV 50 Hz system for electrification in the future.

1957
British Rail's Southern Region introduces diesel-electric multiple units.

1958
The North British Locomotive Company builds Britain's first main-line diesel hydraulic locomotive for British Rail's Western Region.

1959
The first section of 25 kV 50Hz railway in Britain opens on 16 March between Colchester and Walton.
British Rail's last steam locomotive the 2-10-0 Evening Star is completed at Swindon.

1960
The last steam locomotive is withdrawn from Canadian railways in April.
British Rail introduces germanium and silicon rectifiers for railcars and locomotives.
British Rail opens first section of the electrified London Midland Region main line between Crewe and Manchester, using the 25 kV 50 Hz system which is being adopted as standard worldwide.

1961
British Rail introduces rheostat braking for ac locomotives.
Class 73 'electro-diesel' Bo-Bo locomotives delivered to British Rail. These are capable of working on or off a third rail system.

1964
Japan opens a standard-gauge high-speed Shinkansen line from Osaka to Tokyo on 1 October.

1965
The first regular Shinkansen service opens on the Japanese

Shinkansen line in November. The high-speed 'bullet' trains travel at over 100 mph/161km/h.

Electrification is completed on the London-Manchester-Liverpool line.

1968
Steam traction is eradicated from British Rail lines, with the exception of one narrow-gauge line in Wales.

1969
The US Union Pacific Railroad introduces the Do-Do Centennial, the biggest and most powerful ever single-unit diesel-electric locomotive.

1970
China opens the Chengtu-Kunming Railway.

1972
SNCF tests the first prototype TGV, driven by gas-turbine.

1973
A British high-speed diesel takes the diesel traction speed record on 12 June on the Northallerton-Thirsk section of the Darlington-York line. It records a speed of 144mph (232km/h).

The Black Mesa and Lake Powell Railroad in the USA is the first to open using 50kV.

1975
British Rail tests the Advanced Passenger Train between Swindon and Reading. It attains a speed of 152mph (244km/h).

China's first electrified trunk line (25kV 50Hz) opens from Chengtu to Paochi on 1 July.

1976
BR introduces its class 56 Co-Co diesel-electric freight locomotive in May. It has a maximum speed of 81 mph (130km/h)

Chronology of Rail and Steam

British Rail introduces its High Speed Trains (HSTs) on London-Bristol/South Wales route in October.

1978

The Merseyrail system opens in its entirety on 3 January.

HST's are introduced by British Rail on London-Edinburgh route, shortening the journey time to 4hrs and 52mins.

1979

Chinese People's Republic Railways opens the line to Lhasa in Tibet in October.

British Rail's APT (Advanced Passenger Train) achieves a speed of 160mph (257.5 km/h) in Dumfriesshire.

1980

The first part of the Tyne and Wear Metro opens to passengers on 1 August.

1981

The French TGV (Trains à Grande Vitesse) commence a regular hourly service from Paris to Lyons on 27 September.

1982

British Rail takes delivery of its first Class 58 Co-Co diesel-electric freight locomotives.

1983

British Rail sells off its last hotel, the Queen's in Leeds.

1984

On 12 December, British Rail's APT completes the journey from London to Glasgow in 3hrs and 52 mins.

The Dublin Area Rapid Transit opens on 23 July, using the 1.5 kV dc system.

1986

British Rail takes delivery of American Foster Yeoman Class 59 diesel-electric locomotives (built by General Motors) as a result of dissatisfaction with the unreliability of the Class 56 and 58s.

Work resumes on the Channel Tunnel.

British Rail abandons the APT as a result of technical troubles and its tendency to make passengers feel sick, although the tilting train has been developed throughout Europe and has enjoyed great success.

1987

The High Speed Train (HST) achieves a world speed record for a diesel with a speed of 148mph (238km/h).

The House of Commons grants permission for a rail link to Stansted Airport.

The Scottish Office thwarts a Railtrack bid to seek support for a connecting line and rail bridge over the Dornoch Firth which would reduce the distance to the far north.

The Trans-Europe Express ceases operation.

The SNCF commences a TGV service from Paris to the Cote d'Azur in April.

The Docklands Light Railway opens its first section on 31 August.

Class 90 Bo-Bo locomotives built by British Rail Engineering Ltd at Crewe. These locomotives are designed for use on the West Coast line, where they can easily cope with its sharp gradients.

1988

Germany's last main-line steam locomotive retires on 29 October.

TGV Atlantique achieves regular 187mph (300km/h) between Paris and Brittany.

DeutscheBahn claims a new world speed record on 1 May on its Fulda-Wurzburg 'Neubaustrecke'.

Chronology of Rail and Steam

Production ceases at China's Datong locomotive works.

British Rail sells off Traveller's Fare restaurant and buffet facilities.

British Rail Engineerng Limited produces the first Class 91 Bo-Bo, otherwise known as the InterCity 225. The Class 91 is capable of a top speed of 140mph (225km/h), and is meant for push-pull working on the East Coast line.

1989

British Rail takes delivery of Class 60 Co-Co diesel-electric locomotives - built by Brush Traction of Loughborough with revolutionary 'creep' anti-wheelslip mechanism.

British Rail Engineering Ltd is sold off to a private consortium.

The Welsh Vale of Rheidol Railway, the last steam railway belonging to BR, is sold off to the Brecon Mountain Railway.

The longest tunnel in Canada, the Mount MacDonald, is opened by Canadian Pacific on 4 May.

A French TGV Atlantique sets a new world speed record of 300mph (483 km/h).

1990

A French TGV sets yet another speed record on 18 May - 319mph (513km/h). The TGV Atlantique network is completed in September with the new Paris-Tours-Bordeaux-Biarritz services.

British and French tunnellers meet in the Channel Tunnel on 1 December.

1991

The 'Stansted Express' runs for the first time along the new London-Stansted Airport line on 29 January.

Tunnelling completed on the north running tunnel of the Channel tunnel on 24 May; the south tunnel break through is on 28 June.

British Rail's freight service 'Speedlink' is withdrawn following huge losses. Its privately-run replacement goes into receivership the following year.

A double-decked prototype TGV reaches a speed of 199mph (320km/h) in tests in France in November.

The electrification of the East Coast line is completed in July.

1992

British Rail publishes its Passengers Charter, setting out required standards, but without any extra cash input from government to meet them.

Italian Railways completes the last section of its Direttissima line from Rome to Florence.

Spain builds a new Alta Velocidad Espanola (AVE) or high speed line from Madrid to Seville specially for the Expo '92, which thereafter continues to enjoy huge success.

Japan launches its new aluminium-bodied Series 300 train, which just exceeds the average speed of the Paris Montparnasse-Le Mans TGV.

1993

A Russian prototype diesel engine, the TEP80 Bo-Bo + Bo-Bo, claims a world speed record for a diesel train at 161.6mph (260km/h).

New Zealand Railways are bought by a USA consortium lead by Wisconsin Central Ltd, although New Zealand continues to own the railway lands.

Authorization is secured for a London-Heathrow Airport Express link.

The first trains run on the Manchester Airport link on 30 March.

SNCF test a TGV-R train for a new Paris-Brussels service.

The Waterloo and City Railway reopens in London on 19 July.

Swedish Railways test a tilting train set, the X2000, at 171mph (276 km/h).

Chronology of Rail and Steam

Royal Assent is given for the British Rail Privatization Bill on 5 November.

The first French-built Eurostar train passes through the Channel Tunnel for testing. The train is based on the design of the TGV.

1994

The Queen and President Mitterand open the Channel Tunnel on 6 May.

1997

The last British Rail franchise is sold off thereby completing privatization. British Rail ceases to exist.

Preserved, Private and Tourist Railways

Bala Lake Railway, Llanuwchylln, Bala, Gwynedd, Wales. Tel: 016784 666
This railway has 4.4 miles (7km) of 600mm gauge track upon which run ex-slate quarry locomotives. There is also a museum housing a collection of old railway equipment. It was founded in 1972.

Bluebell Railway, Sheffield Park Station, Sheffield Park, Sussex. Tel: 0182 572 3777
A preserved standard gauge passenger line, founded in 1959, with 11 miles (20km) of line upon which run mainly ex-Southern Railway locomotives and rolling stock.

Bo'ness and Kinneil Railway, Bo'ness Station, Union Street, Bo'ness, West Lothian.
This railway was built specially for tourists and enthusiasts in 1979, and runs passenger trains along 3.5 miles (5.5km) of standard gauge track. Its rolling stock includes some locomotives from several Scottish companies as well as the London and North Eastern Railway and British Rail.

Brecon Mountain Railway, Pant Station, Dowlais, near Merthyr Tydfil, South Wales. Tel: 01685 4854
Founded in 1980, this railway runs passenger trains over some 1.9 miles (3km) of 600mm gauge track. Its steam locomotives include some imported from South Africa and Germany.

Preserved, Private and Tourist Railways 180

Bure Valley Railway, Norwich Road, Aylsham, Norfolk. Tel: 01493 655358/657338
This railway was developed in 1989 to provide 8.8 miles (14.3km) of 381mm gauge track. Rides are provided on rolling stock hired from the Romney, Hythe and Dymchurch Railway.

Dean Forest Railway, Norchard Steam Centre, Lydney, Gloucestershire. Tel: 01594 843423
Founded in 1970, this railway has 1 mile (1.6km) of 1435mm gauge track on old colliery lines, and offers passenger rides on a steam train. There is also a museum.

East Lancashire Railway, Bolton Street Station, Bury, Lancashire. Tel: 0161 764 7790
Founded in the early 1980's, this railway offers rides on a passenger train pulled by an Ivatt 2-6-0 (amongst others) along 8.3 miles (13.4km) of standard gauge track.

East Somerset Railway, Cranmore Station, Shepton Mallet, Somerset. Tel: 01749 888 417
Founded in 1973 by the artist David Shepherd, this railway offers steam rides from Cranmore to Mendip Vale along 2 miles (3.2km) of standard gauge track.

Embsay Steam Railway, Embsay Station, Skipton, Yorks.
Tel: 01756 4727/5189
This railway (founded in 1977) has 2.5 miles (4km) of standard gauge line upon which run steam trains for passenger rides. There is also a small museum and mining centre, and a large collection of locomotives.

Fairbourne and Barmouth Railway, Beech Road, Fairbourne, Gwynedd, Wales. Tel: 01341 250362

This narrow gauge (311mm) railway was founded in 1916 and offers trips to the estuary on half-size trains pulled by half-size locomotives. It has approximately 2.2 miles (3.5km) of track.

Ffestiniog Railway and Museum, Harbour Station, Porthmadog, Gwynedd, Wales. Tel: 01766 512340 / 831654
The Ffestiniog is a well known narrow-gauge railway (600mm), running along 12.4 miles (21km) of track amidst glorious mountain and lakeside scenery. The railway has a collection of original steam locomotives and rolling stock.

Foxfield Steam Railway, Blythe Bridge, Stoke-on-Trent. Staffordshire. Tel: 01782 396210
Foxfield Railway has 3.7 miles (6km) of standard gauge track over which run passenger trains hauled by steam locomotives. The old colliery line was opened in 1893; the preserved railway was founded in 1970.

Gloucester and Warwickshire Steam Railway, Toddington Station, Toddington, Gloucestershire. Tel: 0124262 1405
Opened in 1979, this steam railway will have 11.5 miles (21km) of standard-gauge track when the new extension opens on 12 July 1997. Amongst the steam locomotives which haul their passenger trains are two ex-GWR 4-6-0 locomotives.

Great Central Railway, Loughborough Central Station, Great Central Road, Loughborough, Leicestershire. Tel: 01509 230726
This is a preserved main-line railway founded in 1971 with 8 miles (13km) of standard gauge track.

Isle of Man Steam Railway, Strathallan Crescent, Douglas, Isle of Man. Tel: 01624 74549

Preserved, Private and Tourist Railways 182

Daily steam locomotive passenger services still run on the 15 miles (25 km) line which was founded in 1873. The Western terminus at Port Erin has a museum.

Isle of Wight Steam Railway, Haven Street Station, Ryde, Isle of Wight. Tel: 01983 882204
This standard gauge line was re-opened in 1971 and has an interchange with British Rail at Smallbrook Junction station. It has 5 miles (8km) of track.

Keighley and Worth Valley Railway, West Yorkshire, Haworth Station, Keighley, Yorkshire. Tel: 01535 45214
Passenger trains are hauled by steam locomotives from Keighley to Oxenhope further up the valley on 4.4 miles (7km) of standard gauge railway. There is a museum at Oxenhope and Haworth has a locomotive depot and workshops.

Kent and East Sussex Railway, Tenterden Town Station, Tenterden, Kent. Tel: 015806 2943
Founded in 1971, this restored Edwardian steam railway has 7 miles (11km) of standard gauge track and an interesting museum containing Colonel Stephens' memorabilia.

Lakeside and Haverthwaite Railway, Haverthwaite Station, near Ulverston, Cumbria. Tel: 015395 31594
Originally a part of the railway from Furness to Lakeside, this has just over 3 miles (5km) of standard gauge track. It connects with boat cruises on Lake Windermere. It was established in 1960.

Launceston Steam Railway, Newport Industrial Estate, Launceston, Cornwall. Tel: 01566 5665
This railway travels along 2.5 miles (4km) of the old North

Cornwall Railway route on 600mm gauge. It uses old North Wales quarry locomotives and was established in 1982.

Lavender Line, Isfield Station, near Uckfield, East Sussex. Tel: 0182 575 515
Industrial locomotives are used to haul passenger trains along 1.2 miles (2km) of standard gauge track. The line was re-opened in 1993.

Leighton Buzzard Railway, Page's Park Station, Billington road, Leighton Buzzard. Tel: 01525 373888
This narrow-gauge (610mm) railway offers a 3 miles (5km) ride along a line that was originally used to transport sand and gravel to the London and North Western Railway main line from the pits.

Llanberis Lake Railway, Padarn Station, Gilfach Ddu, Llanberis, Gwynedd, Wales. Tel: 01286 870549
A narrow gauge (600mm) line which opened in 1969 to carry passengers along 1.9 miles (3 km) of the old route alongside Llanberis Lake once used by slate trains.

Llangollen Railway, Llangollen Station, Denbighshire, Wales. Tel: 01978 860951
What makes Llangollen different from all the other North Wales preserved lines is that its 5.6miles (9km) of track is standard gauge. It takes passengers from Llangollen to Berwyn and Corwen. It was established in 1981.

Manx Electric Railway, Derby Castle, Douglas, Isle of Man. Tel: 01624 74549
Founded in 1894, this Victorian electric tramway runs on 18 miles (29km) of 914mm gauge using 550V dc. It travels from

Preserved, Private and Tourist Railways 184

Douglas to Ramsey where there is a museum concerned with the island's tramways.

Market Bosworth Light Railway, Shakerstone Station, near Market Bosworth, Leicestershire. Tel 01827 715790
Steam and diesel passenger trains run along 2.5 miles (4km) of standard gauge track towards the Bosworth battlefield. Founded in 1978.

Middleton Railway, Moors Road, Leeds, Yorkshire. Tel: 0113 2710320
Steam passenger trains travel over a total of 1.5 miles (2.4km) standard gauge track where Blenkinsop's engines once worked. Founded in 1959.

Mid-Hants Railway (The Watercress Line), Alresford Station, Alresford, Hampshire. Tel: 01962 722810/734200
Big British and American steam locomotives haul passenger trains (and the very popular Watercress Belle catering train) along 10.6miles (17km) of standard gauge track. Established in 1977.

Nene Valley Railway, Wansford Station, near Peterborough, Cambridgeshire. Tel: 01780 782854
Travel along 7.5 miles (12km) of standard gauge tracks on any of the railway's locomotives and coaches from eleven European and Scandinavian countries. Established in 1974.

North Norfolk Railway, Sheringham Station, Sheringham, Norfolk. Tel: 01263 822045
A standard gauge steam railway which runs along 5.6 miles (9km) of the old Midland and Great Northern joint line. Established in 1969.

North York Moors Railway, Pickering Station, Pickering, Yorkshire. Tel: 01751 72508/73535
Passenger rides on 18 miles (29km) of standard-gauge track over the glorious north Yorkshire Moors. The railway possesses a large collection of locomotives once owned by the London and North Eastern Railway, the London and Manchester Railway, the Great Western Railway and Southern Railways as well as British Rail. Established in 1967.

Ravenglass and Eskdale Railway, Ravenglass Station, Ravenglass, Cumbria. Tel: 01229 717171
A narrow-gauge (381mm) railway through 6.8 miles (11km) of beautiful Lakeland scenery. Founded 1915, re-established 1960.

Romney, Hythe and Dymchurch Railway, New Romney Station, New Romney, Kent. Tel: 01679 62353
This famous narrow-gauge (381mm) railway became a symbol of British resistance to Germany during the Second World War and even ran miniature armoured trains. Rescued in 1971 by a consortium headed by the wealthy 'Bill' McAlpine, the railway now conveys about 150,000 tourists every year in addition to local passengers. It runs for 14.3 miles (23km) along the Kent coast using one third-scale Pacific locomotives.

Severn Valley Railway, The Railway Station, Bewdley, Worcestershire/Shropshire. Tel: 01299 403816
Established in 1965 it has built a new station in Kidderminster in addition to its five other originals. It has 16 miles (26km) of standard gauge run from Bewdley to Kidderminster.

Snaefell Mountain Railway, Laxey, Isle of Man. Tel: 01624 74549
An electrically-powered 1067mm gauge railway, the Sneafell

Preserved, Private and Tourist Railways 186

travels 4.4 miles (7 km) up the mountain to a height of 620.5 metres (2,036ft) where the passenger will see panoramic views across to England, Ireland, Scotland and Wales. Established in 1895, the railway runs on 550V DC, sharing its power supply with the Manx Electric Railway.

Snowdon Mountain Railway, Llanberis, Gwynedd, Wales. Tel: 01286 870223
Travelling on the only rack and pinion system in the country, steam passenger trains climb the 4.5 miles (7.2km) to the summit of Mount Snowdon. Established in 1896.

South Devon Railway, Buckfastleigh Station, Buckfastleigh, Devon. Tel: 01364 642338
A rural branch line, travelling 6.8 miles (11km) on standard gauge along the banks of the River Dart. Railway museum. Established in 1972.

Strathspey Railway, The Station, Boat of Garten, Highland Region. Tel: 0147 983 692
Steam and diesel trains carry passengers along 7.5 miles (12km) of standard gauge track from boat of Garten to Aviemore. Established in 1971.

Swanage Railway, Station House, Swanage, Dorset. Tel: 01929 425800
A 6 mile (10km) standard-gauge railway founded in 1972. It was originally a branch line of the Southern Railway, and there are plans afoot to extend the line to connect it up to the old British Rail line at Wareham.

Tal-y-llyn Railway, Wharf Station, Tywyn, Gwynedd, Wales. Tel: 01654 710472

A narrow-gauge (686mm) line with veteran steam locomotives which runs 7.5 miles (12km) from Tywyn to Nant Gwernol. First opened 1865; reopened in 1950.

Vale of Rheidol Railway, Aberystwyth, Ceredigion, Wales. Tel: 01685 4854
This was the last of British Rail's lines to use steam power. The passenger travels along the mountainside on 23 miles (37km) of standard gauge track in some of the larger and more modern locomotives available to preserved railways. Established in 1902.

Wells and Walsingham Light Railway, Stiffkey Road, Wells-next-the-Sea, Norfolk.
Possibly the world's longest miniature railway, running 4 miles (6.4km) on 260mm gauge track. Opened 1982.

Welshpool and Llanfair Light Railway, Llanfair, Caereinion Station, Llanfair, Powys, Wales. Tel: 01938 8910441
This narrow-gauge (762mm) carries passengers 8 miles (12.8km) along the valley from Llanfair to Welshpool. Established in 1960.

West Somerset Railway, The Railway Station, Minehead, Somerset. Tel: 01643 4996
There are no fewer than ten stations along the 20 miles (31.8km) of preserved railway, which operates large steam locomotives on a standard-gauge track. Most of the steam locomotives are ex-Great Western Railway. Founded in 1974.